Collins

Student Support
Materials for AQA

AS Biology

Unit 2: The Variety of Living Organisms

Author: Mike Boyle

Series Editors: Keith Hirst and Lesley Higginbottom

Published by Collins
An imprint of HarperCollinsPublishers
77-85 Fulham Palace Road
Hammersmith
London
W6 8JB

Browse the complete Collins catalogue at
www.collinseducation.com

© HarperCollinsPublishers Limited 2008

10 9 8 7 6 5 4 3 2 1

ISBN-13 978-0-00-726818-4
ISBN-10 0-00-726818-1

British Library Cataloguing in Publication Data. A Catalogue record for this publication is available from the British Library.

Commissioned by Penny Fowler
Series Editors Keith Hirst and Lesley Higginbottom
Edited by Kath Senior
Proof read by Rachel Hutchings
Design by Newgen Imaging
Cover design by Angela English
Production by Arjen Jansen
Printed and bound in Hong Kong by Printing Express

(a) (i)   (ii)

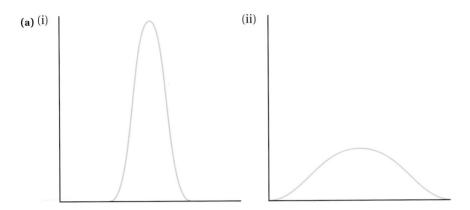

Fig 1
(a) Different normal distribution curves.
   (i) A narrow distribution curve.
   (ii) A wide distribution curve.
The standard deviation in graph (i) is much greater than in graph (ii).

(b)

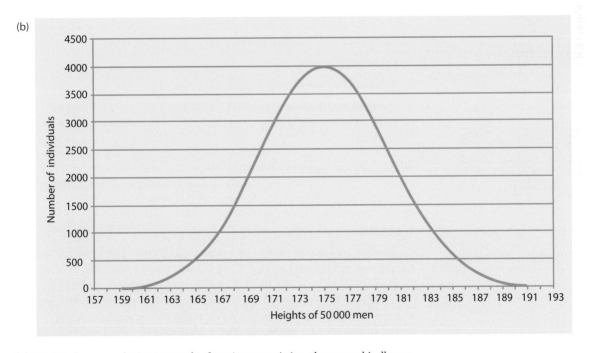

(b) Height in human males is an example of continuous variation, shown graphically as a bell-shaped curve known as a normal distribution. Environment also plays a part; without adequate nutrition and health care, an individual will not reach their full height

Normal distribution, mean and standard deviation

Biological data, such as the height of individuals, usually varies. When such data is plotted on a graph a normal distribution is obtained (see Fig 1a). Most individuals are in the middle, fewer at the extremes.

The **mean** is the arithmetic average. In the example shown in Fig 1a, the mean height is 175 cm.

Standard deviation refers to the spread of the data around the mean, and is shown in the width of the curve. One standard deviation is the range on either side of the mean that contains 68% of the sample, and two standard deviations contain 95% of the sample. In Fig 1b, you would write that the standard deviation in human male height is 175 cm ± 5 cm, which means that 68% of the male population falls in a 10 cm range from 170 to 180 cm.

Causes of variation

Ultimately, mutation is the source of all variation. A gene mutation is a change in the base sequence of the DNA. When a mutated gene is used in **protein synthesis**, there will be a change in the amino acid sequence. The amino acid chain will fold and bend into a differently shaped protein. The change in protein structure is usually harmful or neutral, but occasionally beneficial. Such beneficial mutations give an individual a selective advantage – this is the driving force behind evolution.

Mutation creates new alleles, but there are three more processes that also increase variation in organisms by creating *new combinations of alleles* (see also page 10, for the section on **meiosis**):

1 **Crossover** in meiosis.

2 **Independent assortment** in meiosis.

3 **Random fertilisation** of **gametes** – in animals, all sperm and ova are genetically unique, and which sperm happens to fertilise the egg is totally random.

Investigating variation – twin studies

When studying variation, it is difficult to determine the relative importance of genes and the environment. In humans, a lot of work has been done on identical and non-identical twins, and this is a popular exam topic. The key points are:

1 Identical – or **monozygotic** – twins have exactly the same genotype so any differences between them are likely to be due to environment, in other words, their upbringing. Identical twins reared apart are especially interesting to geneticists. There is also some evidence that random gene expression creates differences. For example, the pattern of moles or freckles on the skin of identical twins is different.

2 Non-identical – or **dizygotic** – twins reared together have different genes but largely the same environment (though it can never be exactly the same). Any differences in these twins are largely genetic.

3 It is difficult to draw valid conclusions from twin studies in humans because there are so few subjects to study. To make the results more reliable we would need random sampling from a large number of individuals, but there just aren't that many. When the group being studied is so small, chance plays a big part in contributing to differences between samples.

Essential Notes

It's a bit like a pack of playing cards. Mutation creates new cards, and the three other processes shuffle the pack.

3.2.2 DNA is an information-carrying molecule. Its sequence of bases determines the structure of proteins, including enzymes

The properties and structure of DNA

DNA is a remarkable molecule with two key abilities:

- It carries information – the **genetic code** – from which the essential proteins are made. This process is called protein synthesis.

- It can make exact copies of itself, time after time. This process is called **DNA replication**. Without this ability there would be no cell division and therefore no growth, repair or reproduction.

DNA is a **nucleic acid**, so called because it is found in the nucleus and is weakly acidic. It is a stable **polynucleotide**. Stable because it does not start to denature until heated to a temperature of about 90 °C; polynucleotide because it is made from many **nucleotide** units. DNA is much more stable than proteins, many of which begin to denature around 40–50 °C.

DNA molecules are enormous – the largest molecules you are ever likely to study. If a single human **chromosome** were stretched out it could be up to 5 cm long, when most molecules are measured in nanometres. Obviously DNA never gets stretched out because it remains locked away inside the nucleus, and therefore must be coiled up.

In **eukaryotic cells** the DNA is linear and attached to organising proteins called **histones**, like cotton round a bobbin, as seen in Fig 2. In **prokaryotic cells** (bacteria) the DNA is organised in a completely different way; it is circular (in a loop) and not attached to histones.

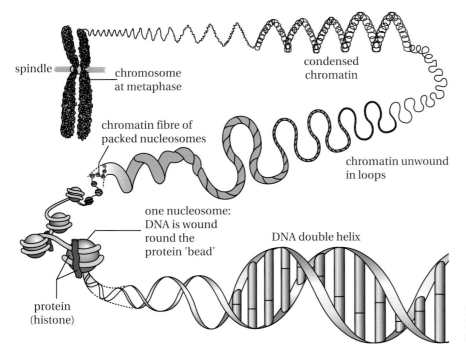

spindle

chromosome at metaphase

condensed chromatin

chromatin fibre of packed nucleosomes

chromatin unwound in loops

one nucleosome: DNA is wound round the protein 'bead'

DNA double helix

protein (histone)

Fig 2
Each chromosome is one long supercoiled DNA molecule

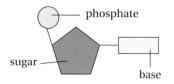

Fig 3
The basic structure of a nucleotide

DNA is a **polymer**: the monomers are nucleotides. As Fig 3 shows, each nucleotide has three components:

- a **sugar** – deoxyribose – which is a 5-carbon sugar

- a **phosphate** (PO_4^{3-}) molecule

- a **base** – one of four nitrogen-containing compounds – adenine (A), thymine (T), guanine (G) or cytosine (C).

The nucleotides are arranged in a double helix – a twisted ladder (Fig 2). The two sides of the ladder are chains of alternating sugar-phosphate groups, while the 'rungs' are made from pairs of bases bonded together by hydrogen bonds. For both protein synthesis and replication, it is important that the strands can separate and rejoin without damaging the molecule. Only one part of one strand of the DNA at any particular point in the double-stranded molecule – the **sense strand** – is used to make proteins. The other side serves to stabilise the molecule. The sense strand for different genes may be found on different sides of the molecule.

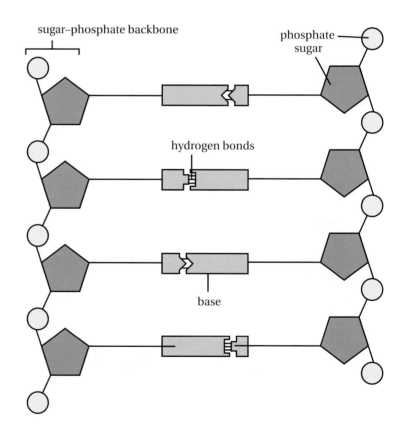

Fig 4
Nucleotides are joined by condensation reactions to form a single DNA chain, which bonds with a complementary DNA chain. These chains twist together to make a double helix. The covalent bonds between the sugar and phosphate groups are much stronger than hydrogen bonds

The bases in a DNA molecule
The four bases in a DNA molecule always bond in the same way – A to T and C to G. So if you know the base sequence down one side of the DNA molecule, you can predict the sequence on the other.

For example:

If one side reads   CGCGTTAATACGC

the other side will read GCGCAATTATGCG

The bases are held together by hydrogen bonds, two between A and T (A=T) and three between C and G (G≡C). These regular hydrogen bonds along the whole length of the molecule make DNA very stable.

What are genes?

The definition of a gene is central to this topic. **A gene is a section of DNA (deoxyribonucleic acid) that codes for the manufacture of a particular polypeptide or protein**.

The position of a particular gene on a chromosome is known as its **locus**. The plural of locus is **loci**. Different versions of genes are called alleles, and they arise by **mutation**. A fault in the copying of the base sequence in a particular gene will probably change the amino acid sequence, which, in turn, will produce a different **polypeptide**/protein. These slightly altered proteins may function as normal, but it is also possible that they will not work, and this will cause problems in the organism. A non-functional enzyme may cause a metabolic block, which can result in the death of the organism.

Genes and polypeptides

Basically, genes have the code the cell needs to make polypeptides, and a complete protein consists of one or more polypeptides. Proteins control the growth and development of the organism. But, how does the cell use the information coded in the genes to make particular proteins?

A gene consists of a particular sequence of bases, for example CTTATTCCGTTT. A polypeptide consists of a particular sequence of amino acids, for example, val-his-glu-ser-pro. So, how does a gene code for a polypeptide?

There are just 4 different bases but 20 different amino acids. It can't be one base = one amino acid, nor can it be two bases: there are $4 \times 4 = 16$ different two-base combinations, which is still not enough. So it has to be three bases.

A sequence of three bases, called a **triplet**, codes for one particular amino acid. For example, the DNA triplet TAC codes for the amino acid methionine.

NB The details about protein synthesis, including how the different types of RNA are involved, comes in the A2 course.

As Fig 5 overleaf shows, genes occur at particular places along a DNA molecule. There is a lot of non-coding DNA in between the genes, which may or may not have an important function – it's just another aspect of the human **genome** that we don't yet fully understand. Often the non-coding DNA consists of the same base sequence occurring again and again, known as **multiple repeats**, and the differences in this non-coding DNA form the basis of DNA profiling in forensics.

The genes themselves also contain some non-coding DNA. These base sequences do not contribute to the polypeptide, and are called **introns**. When a gene is transcribed the intron must be removed, leaving only the sequences to be expressed – the **exons**.

Examiners' Notes

Practise predicting the sequence of bases along a strand of DNA from the sequence on the opposite strand.

Examiners' Notes

Learn the definition of a gene. You may have been taught that genes control features such as eye colour and hair colour but in reality *genes make proteins* (including lots of different enzymes). It is those proteins that make the hair and eye colour, and all the other observable features that contribute to our genotype.

Examiners' Notes

You will never have to learn any examples of particular triplets and their amino acids – the exam questions will always provide them for you.

Fig 5
Even in a gene, there are non-coding lengths of DNA called introns. Only the extons are encoded into the mRNA molecule, and therefore expressed

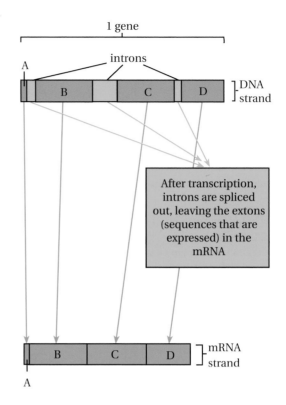

After transcription, introns are spliced out, leaving the extons (sequences that are expressed) in the mRNA

Examiners' Notes

Make sure you understand the difference between homologous (as in chromosome) and homozygous (as in gene).

Essential Notes

The bands on the chromosomes in the figure are not individual genes. Different sections of DNA take up stains in different amounts making it look banded.

Examiners' Notes

Many candidates lose marks by stating that all organisms have 23 pairs of chromosomes. Never mention the number 23 unless the question is specifically about humans.

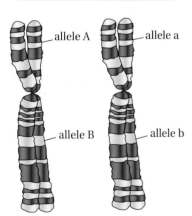

Fig 6
In diploid cells, chromosomes occur in pairs so that every cell has two alleles of each gene. Note that the bands are not all alleles. The bands just appear when the chromosomes are stained, the alleles are much smaller.

Meiosis

First, four vital definitions:

- **Diploid** = A cell/organism which contains two sets of chromosomes. It is written as 2n. For example, in humans 2n = 46. Different species have different numbers of chromosomes

- **Haploid** = A cell/organism which contains a single set of chromosomes. Shown as n, e.g. n = 23

- **Mitosis** = Cell division in which cells are copied. One diploid cell gives rise to two identical diploid cells (or, more rarely, one haploid cell gives rise to two haploid cells)

- **Meiosis** = Cell division that shuffles the genes on the chromosomes so that all cells produced are genetically different. One diploid cell gives rise to *four* haploid cells.

You can see from the last definition that there are two key features to meiosis:

- It creates genetic variation

- It halves the number of chromosomes in the cell.

It is therefore completely different from mitosis, which does neither. Let's look at it in more detail, using humans as an example

Every diploid human cell has 23 pairs of chromosomes. These pairs are **homologous**, which is another way of saying they have the same genes in the same positions but the alleles of those genes may differ. This is shown in Fig 6.

Meiosis is illustrated in Fig 7 overleaf.

Early in the first meiotic division, homologons chromosomes pair up and lie alongside each other.

Crossover takes place. *Chiasmata* form and *blocks of genes* are *swapped* between material and paternal chromosomes.

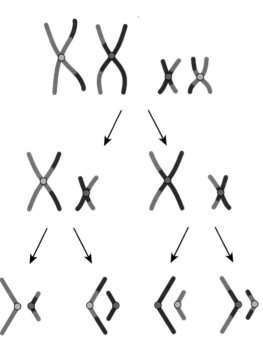

Result of crossover: each chromosome now has *new allele combinations*

FIRST MEIOTIC DIVISION
Independent assortment has taken place: are from each pair has gone into the daughter cell. The combination shown is just 1 of the 2 possible.

SECOND MEIOTIC DIVISION
The chromatids have been pulled apart, as in mitosis. End result: 4 daughter cells, all haploid, all genetically unique.

Fig 7
An overview of meiosis showing two pairs of homologous chromosomes

Meiosis produces variation in two ways:

1 In **crossover**, blocks of genes are swapped between homologous chromosomes (Fig 8). This produces variation because the crossover points – called **chiasmata** – occur at random. The result is that, although each chromosome still has a full set of genes, it may well have *new and different combinations of alleles*. This prevents the same set of alleles being passed down unchanged from generation to generation.

2 **Independent assortment** – the haploid cells contain *one* member from each homologous chromosome pair, but the choice of which member is purely random. In a cell with 23 pairs of chromosomes, there are 2^{23} different combinations of chromosomes, which is over 8 million.

Examiners' Notes

Don't confuse meiosis with mitosis. Remember: **Meiosis Makes Eggs In Ovaries, Sperm In Scrotum**. (It's not strictly true for all types of organism, but it does help to focus the mind.)

a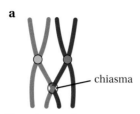

chiasma

b

c

Homologous chromosomes lie alongside each other. They joint at points called chiasmata (singular = chiasma)

When the chromosomes separate blocks of genes have been swapped between maternal and paternal chromosomes. New combinations of alleles have been created.

The homologous chromosomes are pulled apart, and one goes to each daughter cell.

Fig 8
Crossover takes place during the first meiotic division.

3.2.3 Similarities and differences in DNA results in genetic diversity

As we have already seen, differences in organisms are due to:

- differences in their DNA
- differences in the way in which that DNA is expressed.

In this section we look at two forces that can have an effect on genetic **diversity**:

- **Artificial selection**, or selective breeding, in which humans try to improve the quality of various species by breeding together those individuals that show desirable features
- **Bottlenecks** and the **founder effect**. When populations are small, chance plays a significant role in genetics.

Artificial selection (selective breeding)

For generations humans have been improving the quality of their crops and farm animals by selective breeding. The idea is simple: take the individual animals with the most desirable features and breed them together. You don't need a knowledge of DNA, genes or chromosomes, just a basic understanding of the biology of that organism.

In this way we have produced many strains of farm animals and crop plants that are unrecognisable from their wild ancestors. Cows have been selectively bred for milk production, chickens capable of accelerated egg production or rapid growth, wheat that can withstand the cold, pigs that put on weight quickly, the list goes on.

The problems with selective breeding
The main problem with selective breeding is the effect of **inbreeding**. Inevitably, when closely related individuals breed, this reduces genetic variation. Closely related individuals tend to share many of the same genes, including any faulty alleles, which might be paired up and expressed if these individuals mate. This is a well-known problem with **pedigree** animals. For many years a high proportion of Siamese cats were born with a squint and/or kink in their tail at birth.

Problems also occur in bulldogs – many of these pedigree dogs are born with breathing difficulties. We can use this example to explore what is happening at the level of the genome.

Suppose that bulldogs usually have the **dominant** gene T, for normal **trachea** development, but that affected bulldogs have the **recessive** allele t. Possession of the t allele leads to underdevelopment of the trachea, with consequent breathing difficulties.

In a large, randomly breeding population, two Tt individuals would be unlikely to mate. However, in the highly selected population of pedigree bulldogs it is quite likely that a mating will take place between two dogs with the genotype Tt. Their litter of puppies will contain some puppies with genotype tt, which are very likely to have severe breathing difficulties from birth.

Breeders, of course, point out that they carefully study pedigree charts (Fig 9) to minimise the chance of this, and other problems, happening. But, if the normal gene is completely dominant, it masks the presence of the recessive allele in a **heterozygous** bulldog, so the breeders cannot tell if they are risking **homozygous** recessive puppies by breeding two heterozygotes together.

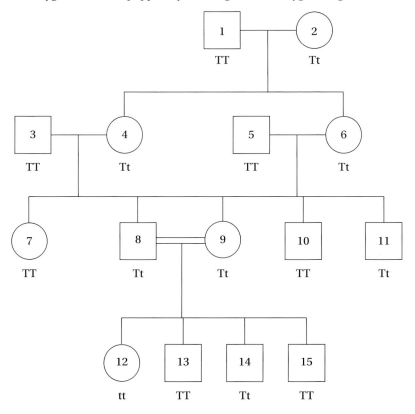

Fig 9
Individual 2 has a copy of the faulty allele t. They will not suffer from the problem because they also have one healthy allele. Both the offspring 4 and 6 are carriers too: they are heterozygotes. The key feature here is that individual 9 is bred with her uncle. Individual 12 has two faulty alleles and therefore inherits the condition.

To summarise:

- Inbreeding promotes **homozygosity** – it is more likely that offspring are TT or tt (tt individuals will suffer from the defect)

- Outbreeding promotes **heterozygosity** – it is more likely that offspring are Tt.

The ethics of selective breeding

Inbreeding can lead to a much higher percentage of abnormalities than random mating, and this creates a lot of unnecessary suffering. For example:

- Modern pigs have been bred to grow extra fast – some breeds now grow so fast their hearts cannot keep up, causing discomfort when the animals are active

- Broiler chickens are also bred to grow fast – some now grow so fast that their skeleton and joints can't develop at the same pace as their muscle, so that they are unable to walk properly.

Conversely, selective breeding can benefit animals:

- It can improve resistance to disease

- Breeding can be done to remove characteristics that cause injury, for example, selecting cattle without horns.

Of course, the overall point of selective breeding is usually to benefit humans. For example:

- More efficient food production. A chicken can go from hatching to chilling on a supermarket shelf in just 35 days

- Lower prices. Such a chicken may cost just two or three pounds.

Some people are uncomfortable with this. Many chickens are reared in very cramped conditions, which saves space and prevents them from wasting energy on movement, so that they put on weight faster, but this is not nice for the chickens. There are ethical guidelines that say the selectively bred animals should be no worse off than the parent stock had they not been manipulated. However, there will always be a conflict between the welfare needs of the animal and the economic viability of food production.

The founder effect

The founder effect is seen when a new population is established by a small number of individuals, which carry only a small fraction of the original population's genetic variation. As a result, the new population may be distinctively different from its parent population, both genetically and phenotypically (Fig 10).

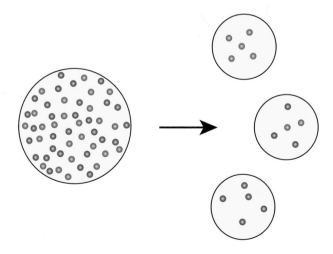

Fig 10
A simple illustration of founder effect. The original population is on the left with three possible founder populations on the right. These are all very different from each other, and from the parent population

Genetic bottlenecks

Genetic bottlenecks occur when a large proportion of a population is killed or otherwise prevented from reproducing, and then recovers from just a few individuals. Cheetahs are a classic example. All of the world's cheetahs are thought to have arisen from a small population in central Africa that narrowly escaped extinction. All of today's cheetahs are virtually identical, showing less variation than between any two human siblings.

3.2.4 **The variety of life is extensive and this is reflected in similarities and differences in its biochemical basis and cellular organisation**

Haemoglobin (Hb)

Haemoglobin is a protein with several important properties:

- It occurs in red blood cells (Fig 11), where it has a vital role in oxygen transport

- It is a protein with a quaternary structure because it is made from four polypeptide chains (Fig 12)

- It has the remarkable ability to pick up oxygen where it is abundant (the lungs) and release it where it is needed (the respiring **tissues**).

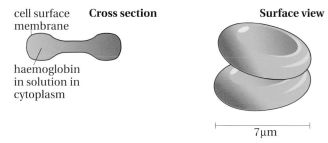

cell surface membrane   **Cross section**   **Surface view**

haemoglobin in solution in cytoplasm

7 μm

Fig 11
Red blood cells. The biconcave shape of the red cell is an efficient compromise between the maximum volume of a sphere and the maximum surface area of a flat disc. This allows the cells to carry a useful amount of oxygen, but to load and unload it quickly

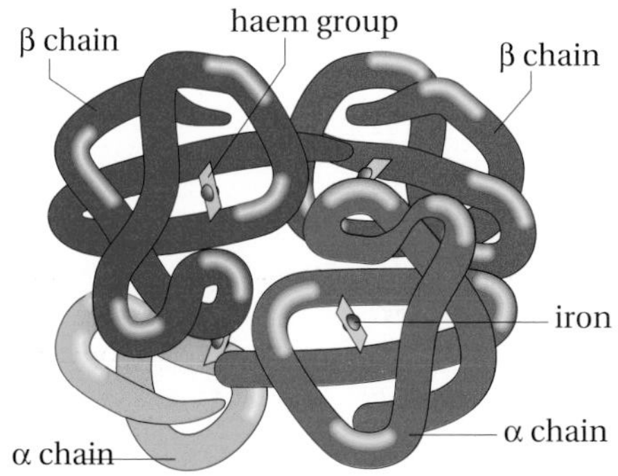

β chain   haem group   β chain

iron

α chain   α chain

Fig 12
The haemoglobin molecule consists of 4 polypeptide chains, two α globins and two β globins. Each chain is attached to a haem group featuring a central iron (Fe^{2+}) ion that combines with an oxygen molecule

Oxygen is carried mainly as oxyhaemoglobin in the red blood cells. As the equation below shows, each haemoglobin molecule can combine with four oxygen molecules:

$$Hb + 4O_2 \rightleftharpoons HbO_8$$
haemoglobin   oxygen   oxyhaemoglobin

A key point about haemoglobin is not that it can pick up oxygen – lots of substances can do that – but that it can release it again in areas where it is needed. The behaviour of haemoglobin with oxygen is illustrated by the **oxygen dissociation curve** (Fig 13).

There are two key features of the oxygen dissociation curve.

1   At the high oxygen concentrations found in the lungs, where the curve is level, haemoglobin becomes almost fully saturated with oxygen.

2   At the low oxygen concentration found in the tissues, where the curve is steep, oxyhaemoglobin dissociates, releasing much of its oxygen. In this part of the curve, a small drop in oxygen concentration can cause a relatively large change in the percentage saturation of the haemoglobin, which releases large amounts of oxygen.

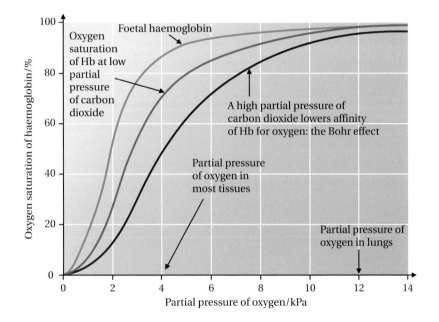

Examiners' Notes

Make sure that you can use the oxygen dissociation curve to predict a change in the percentage saturation of haemoglobin. An exam question could ask you, for example, to predict the change when the partial pressure changes from 4 kPa to 12 kPa. For the foetal curve, for example, it would be 18% (98% at 12 minus 80% at 12).

Fig 13
The oxygen dissociation curve and the Bohr effect

At a higher concentration of carbon dioxide, the curve is shifted to the right. This is because carbon dioxide is an acidic gas that *lowers the **affinity** of haemoglobin for oxygen*. This is known as the **Bohr effect**. The significance of this is seen in metabolically active tissues, such as muscles; the harder they are working, the more carbon dioxide they produce and the more oxygen is released by the haemoglobin.

The steps involved in the release of oxygen at the tissues are shown in Fig 14 and listed below:

1   Carbon dioxide diffuses out of the respiring cell, through the **plasma** and into the red blood cell.

2   The enzyme **carbonic anhydrase** catalyses the reaction between carbon dioxide and water, speeding up the production of carbonic acid, which dissociates into H^+ ions and HCO_3^- (hydrogen carbonate) ions.

3   The H^+ ions combine with haemoglobin, causing the release of the oxygen.

4   The free oxygen molecules diffuse into the respiring cells.

5   The HCO_3^- ions diffuse into the plasma. This causes the red cell to develop a slight positive charge. To counteract this, Cl^- ions flow into the red cell. This is known as the chloride shift.

Most carbon dioxide is transported as HCO_3^- in the plasma.

Examiners' Notes

It is important to distinguish between the *production* of HCO_3^- in the red cells, and the *transport* of HCO_3^- in the plasma.

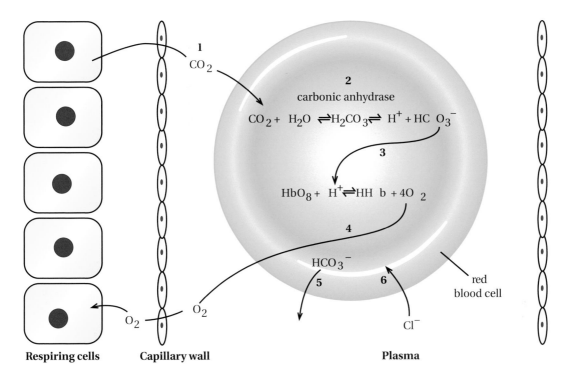

Respiring cells   **Capillary wall**   **Plasma**

Fig 14
Steps in the release of oxygen at the tissues

Haemoglobin across the animal kingdom

Many aquatic invertebrates also make use of haemoglobin. There is much less oxygen in water than in air, and the warmer the water, the less oxygen it can hold. In polluted water oxygen can be especially scarce because the bacteria also compete for what little there is. The following species all owe their red colouration to the presence of haemoglobin.

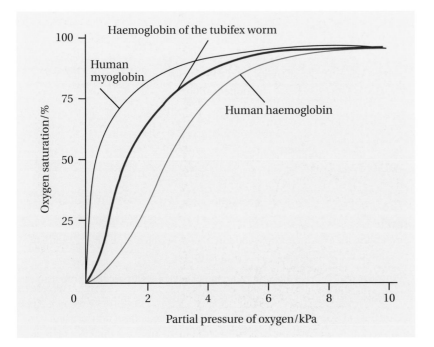

Fig 15
The oxygen dissociation curve for haemoglobin from the tubifex worm lies to the left of the curve for human haemoglobin. This shows that tubifex haemoglobin has a higher affinity for oxygen than human haemoglobin

- **Tubifex** worms live in poorly oxygenated mud at the bottom of rivers and ponds. They burrow head first into the mud, leaving their tails sticking out. The oxygen dissociation curve for tubifex worms is shown in Fig 15.

- **Chironomid midge larvae (bloodworms)** live in burrows, also in poorly oxygenated mud. They must come out from time to time to replenish their oxygen stores. The haemoglobin in their tissues allows them to store oxygen and stay in the burrow for longer, thus avoiding predators.

Carbohydrates

Carbohydrates are an important food source and they also have structural functions in plants and animals. Complex carbohydrates are polymers, made up of repeating sugar, or saccharide units. They are also called polysaccharides. There are three polysaccharides you need to know about:

- **starch**

- **glycogen**

- **cellulose**

These are all polymers, formed from hundreds or thousands of glucose units. Starch and glycogen are made from α glucose while cellulose is made from β glucose.

In Unit 1 we looked at the structure of α glucose. β glucose is very similar, only the position of one –OH group is different. Fig 16 shows the difference, and shows how two glucose molecules join to form a disaccharide.

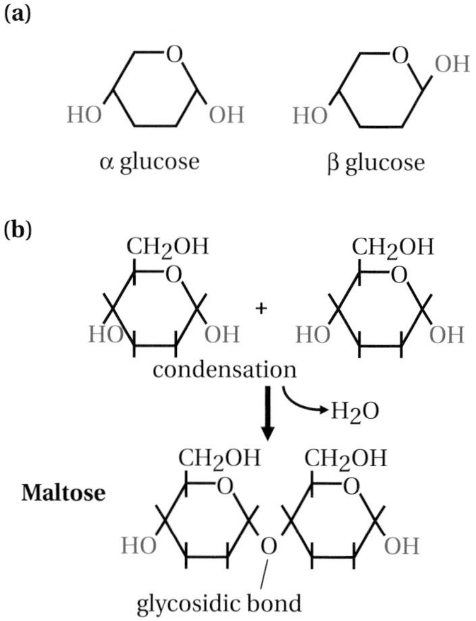

Fig 16
(a) The structure of α and β glucose
(b) Two α glucose molecules combine by condensation to form maltose. This reaction is repeated many times to form polysaccharides

(a)

α glucose   β glucose

(b)

CH$_2$OH   CH$_2$OH

condensation

H$_2$O

Maltose

CH$_2$OH   CH$_2$OH

glycosidic bond

Starch

Starch is the main storage compound in plants. Starch is actually a mixture of two compounds, **amylose** and **amylopectin** (Fig 17).

- Amylose consists of single, unbranched chains of α glucose that form a spiral.

- Amylopectin consists of branched chains of α glucose molecules.

NB Amylase enzymes remove disaccharides from the ends of amylose and amylopectin. This is why starch is hydrolysed to maltose, not directly to glucose.

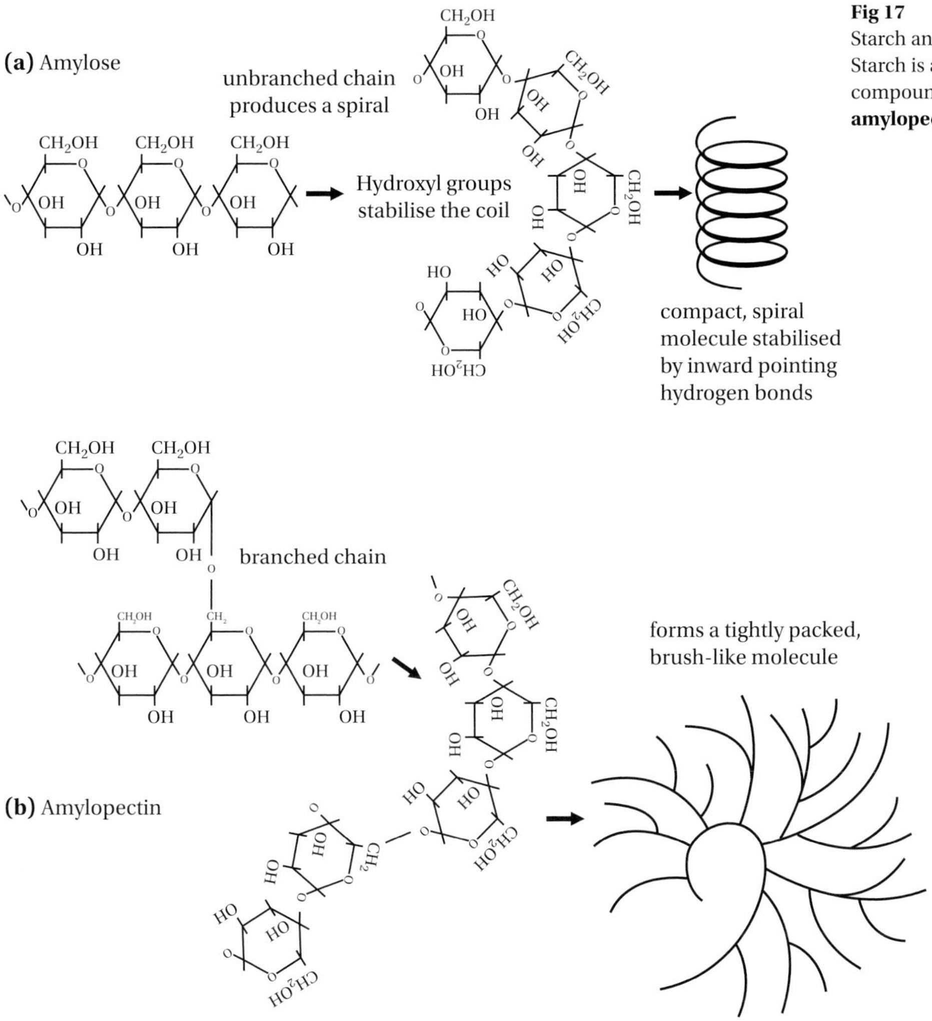

Fig 17
Starch and glycogen
Starch is a mixture of two compounds, **amylose** and **amylopectin**.

(a) Amylose

unbranched chain produces a spiral

Hydroxyl groups stabilise the coil

compact, spiral molecule stabilised by inward pointing hydrogen bonds

(b) Amylopectin

branched chain

forms a tightly packed, brush-like molecule

Storage compounds need to be insoluble, compact and easily converted to energy. The large size of amylose and amylopectin molecules means that they are insoluble, so they do not have an osmotic effect (cause movement of water) in starch-containing cells. The spiral/branched structure of the molecules means that they are compact. The glucose in these compounds can only be released from the ends of the chain. As amylopectin has many branches, it is able to release glucose more quickly than amylose.

Glycogen and cellulose

Glycogen is the main storage carbohydrate in mammals. It is very similar in structure to amylopectin, but is even more branched and so can be built up and broken down even more quickly, matching the greater energy demands of animals.

Cellulose strengthens plant cell walls. It is made only from β glucose molecules (Fig 18 overleaf). This slight difference in structure means that instead of forming a spiral, the β glucose chains are long and straight. When these chains lie parallel to each other, many hydrogen bonds form along the length so that the individual cellulose chains are bound together into strong **microfibrils.** These are then incorporated into plant **cell walls.**

Examiners' Notes

Practise drawing the formation of maltose from two glucose molecules, and make sure you can label the glycosidic bond.

Cellulose is the most abundant polysaccharide on Earth and many familiar materials, such as cotton, paper and nail varnish, owe their strength to cellulose. However, most animals cannot digest it because they do not possess the enzyme **cellulase**. Herbivores have microbes (bacteria and/or **protoctists**) in their guts, which do make cellulase, to help them to digest cellulose.

Fig 18
Cellulose consists of long parallel chains of β glucose molecules. Hydrogen bonds and other weak attractive forces all along the length bind the chains together into strong fibrils

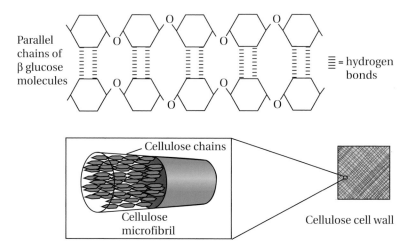

Plant cells

In Unit 1 we saw the basic structure of an animal cell. Like animal cells, plant cells have a nucleus, mitochondria, cell membrane and cytoplasm. They also have a few extra features:

- **A cell wall** – a tough layer made of cellulose, which surrounds plant cells
- A **vacuole** – a large, membrane-bound organelle, which usually contains fluid
- **Chloroplasts** – organelles that contain chlorophyll and that are the site of photosynthesis.

A typical plant cell

Palisade mesophyll cells are typical plant cells (Fig 19). They are found in leaves and are adapted for photosynthesis.

Adaptations in plant cells

Some plant cells have specialised functions, and this is reflected by their structure (Fig 20).

The cell wall

The cell wall is secreted by the plant cell itself. As Fig 18 shows, the long cellulose molecules are arranged into **microfibrils**, which become cemented into the cell wall using a 'glue' that consists of **hemicelluloses** (short chains of glucose molecules).

The wall, which resembles fibreglass when observed under the electron microscope, has several functions:

- It gives the plant cell rigidity and strength.
- It prevents the cell from swelling and bursting due to water intake. The **protoplast** inside the cell swells and pushes against the cell wall until no

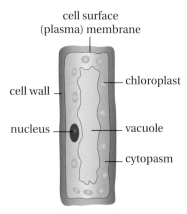

Palisade cell

Fig 19
A palisade mesophyll cell, as seen under the optical (or light) microscope, shows many features typical of plant cells. These cells are adapted for photosynthesis and are packed with chloroplasts. Their deep, cylindrical shape means that they can be packed tightly together to maximise light absorption

further expansion is possible, like a bladder in a football. In this state the cell is said to be **turgid**.

- In multicellular plants, this turgidity gives mechanical strength to the tissues.
- It gives the cell a particular shape. A good example of this is seen in **xylem** fibres, when the cytoplasm in the young xylem vessel dies, leaving just the cell walls to conduct water and dissolved mineral ions up the plant.

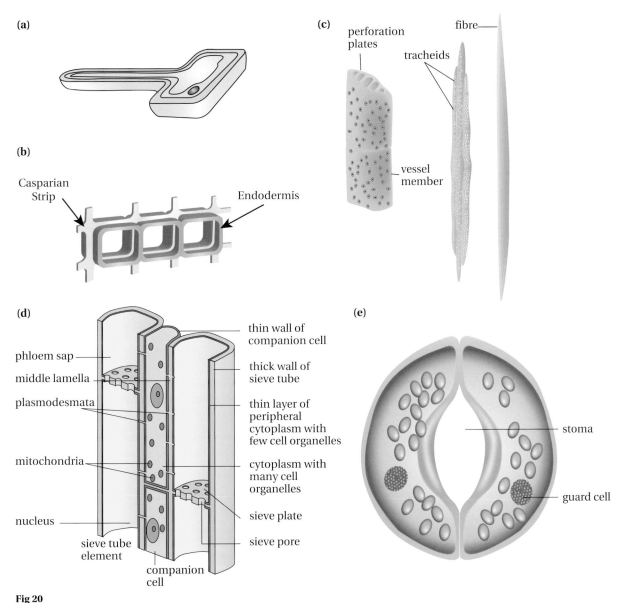

Fig 20
Some specialised plant cells
(a) Root hair cell – projects into the soil and provides a large surface area for the absorption of water and mineral ions
(b) Endodermal cell with Casparian strip – controls the entry of water and minerals into the xylem
(c) Xylem – specialised conducting cells, with strengthened walls and hollow ends that provide a continuous pathway for water transport
(d) Phloem – transports sugars and other organic materials around the plant
(e) Guard cell – can change shape to open or close the stomata

Chloroplasts

Chloroplasts are organelles that contain all the pigments, enzymes and other substances needed for photosynthesis. They are found mainly in the palisade cells of the leaf. Fig 21 shows the ultrastructure of chloroplasts. Key features include:

- A large internal surface area so that as much chlorophyll as possible comes into contact with light

- A flattened shape to enable rapid **diffusion** of substances in and out.

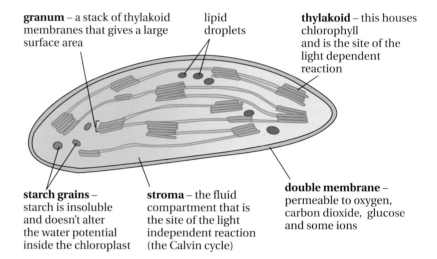

granum – a stack of thylakoid membranes that gives a large surface area

lipid droplets

thylakoid – this houses chlorophyll and is the site of the light dependent reaction

Fig 21
Chloroplasts take the form of flattened discs, rather like Smarties™ (but don't call them that in the exam)

starch grains – starch is insoluble and doesn't alter the water potential inside the chloroplast

stroma – the fluid compartment that is the site of the light independent reaction (the Calvin cycle)

double membrane – permeable to oxygen, carbon dioxide, glucose and some ions

---

3.2.5 **During the cell cycle, genetic information is copied and passed to genetically identical daughter cells**

Replication of DNA

The existence of a molecule that can store information and copy itself is essential to life. If this did not happen, characteristics could not be passed on from generation to generation. But how does DNA copy itself?

In DNA replication the two strands come apart, and each one acts as a template for the addition of complementary nucleotides (Fig 22 overleaf).

The basic process of replication involves these steps:

1. **Helicase** enzymes unwind the two strands of the DNA helix, breaking the hydrogen bonds and separating the two strands.

2. DNA binding proteins attach to keep the strands apart.

3. Primase enzymes add **primers**; short sections of nucleotides that signal to the polymerase enzyme where to begin copying.

4. **DNA polymerase** enzymes attach to the primers and then move along the exposed strands, catalysing the addition of complementary nucleotides to complete the new strands.

5. Mistakes do occur, when the wrong base is inserted, but most of them are corrected by **proofreading** enzymes. Those that are not corrected can lead to mutations.

(a)

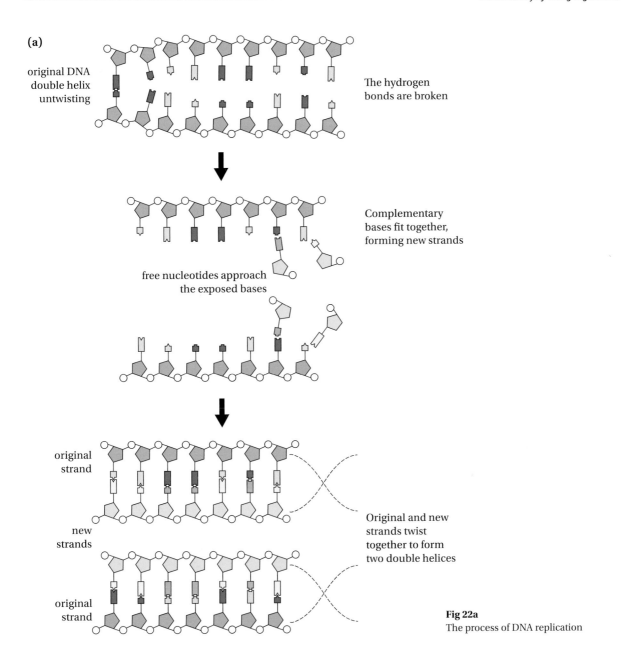

original DNA
double helix
untwisting

The hydrogen
bonds are broken

free nucleotides approach
the exposed bases

Complementary
bases fit together,
forming new strands

original
strand

new
strands

original
strand

Original and new
strands twist
together to form
two double helices

Fig 22a
The process of DNA replication

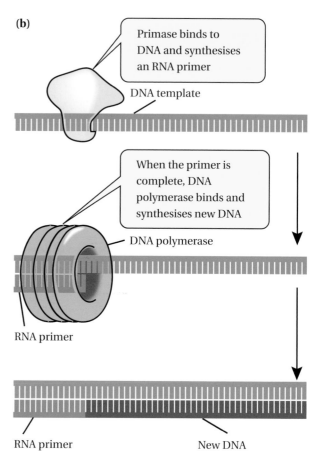

(b)

Primase binds to DNA and synthesises an RNA primer

DNA template

When the primer is complete, DNA polymerase binds and synthesises new DNA

DNA polymerase

RNA primer

RNA primer   New DNA

Fig 22b
DNA replication showing the action of primers

DNA replication is **semi-conservative** because in each daughter DNA molecule one strand is original (it has been conserved) and the other strand is new.

Evidence for the semi-conservative theory of DNA replication

Strong support for the idea that DNA replication is semi-conservative came from a series of classic experiments performed by Meselson and Stahl in the 1950s.

They used an isotope of nitrogen, ^{15}N (heavy nitrogen), that can be incorporated into DNA instead of the normal isotope, ^{14}N, without harming the organism. However, this makes the DNA slightly denser and so DNA containing ^{14}N can be separated from that containing ^{15}N by centrifugation (Fig 23). In this way they were able to show that each new DNA molecule contains one original strand and one new strand.

Exam questions often feature Meselson and Stahl's experiment and ask candidates to predict the bands obtained in the second and third generations.

You may get diagrams in which the two original 'heavy' strands are labelled, and be asked to predict what will happen next. Remember that in each of the generations that follow, there will only be two of these heavy strands.

- In generation 0 there will be one piece of DNA, which will have two heavy strands.

- In generation 1 there will be two pieces of DNA, both hybrid, so one heavy strand and one light strand.

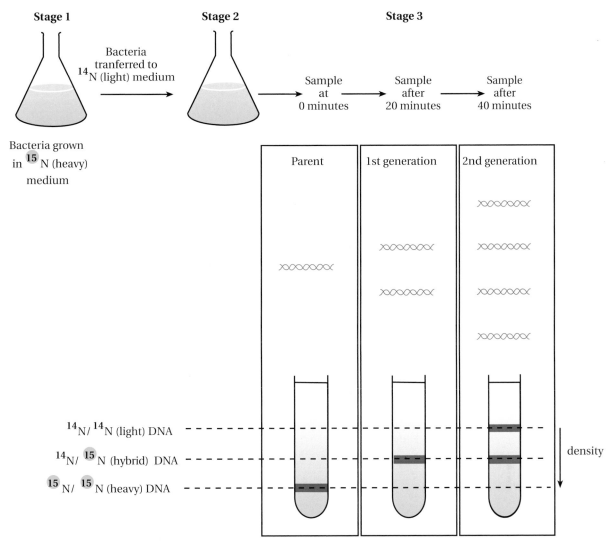

Fig 23
An outline of Meselson and Stahl's experiment.

- In generation 2 there will be four pieces of DNA, two hybrid and two all new.
- In generation 3 there will be eight pieces of DNA, two hybrid and six all new.

And in each subsequent generation there will be two hybrid strands, which will eventually be far outnumbered by the all-new strands.

You might also be given diagrams of tubes. Remember that DNA with two labelled (15 N) strands is the heaviest, followed by DNA with one labelled strand, and DNA with no labelled strands is the lightest or least dense.

The cell cycle

The cell cycle is a series of events that start with the beginning of mitosis and ends when mitosis starts again in the daughter cell. The cycle therefore includes:

- The four phases of mitosis: **prophase**, **metaphase**, **anaphase** and **telophase**.
- The three phases of **interphase**, G1, S and G2.

The stages of mitosis are shown in Fig 24 overleaf.

Examiners' Notes

The stages of mitosis – interphase, prophase, metaphase, anaphase and telophase – can be remembered with the mnemonic IPMAT.

Remembering that meta = middle and that ana = apart makes these stages easy to identify.

When interpreting diagrams or photographs, you can work out the stage of mitosis by the appearance of the chromosomes:

- two long strands = prophase
- two short strands and in the middle of the cell = metaphase
- short single strands near to the equator = anaphase
- single strands near to poles (or if the cell has started to divide) = telophase.

Mitosis

Mitosis is 'straightforward' cell division in which the DNA replicates and the cell splits to form two new cells. Each daughter cell receives an exact copy of the original DNA (unless there is a mutation). Organisms grow and repair themselves by mitosis.

Mitosis produces two daughter cells with identical genetic information: these cells are **clones** of the original cell. Before it divides by mitosis, a cell must first duplicate all of its DNA, and then organise the division so that each new cell gets a full set. DNA replication takes place *before* cell division, during interphase, while the DNA is spread out rather than condensed into chromosomes.

When DNA is spread out and diffuse in the nucleus, it is known as **chromatin**. Early in cell division the DNA condenses into chromosomes. The word chromosome means 'coloured body'. When chromosomes condense, they appear as double structures (Fig 25). This is a consequence of DNA replication. Each part of the chromosome – known as a **chromatid** – is identical. The two chromatids are held together by a **centromere**.

Interphase is the period of time between the start of one round of cell division and the start of the next. Most cells are in interphase most of the time. The chromosomes of cells in interphase are not visible because the DNA is spread out, and some of the genes are being **expressed** (translation is taking place and proteins are being produced).

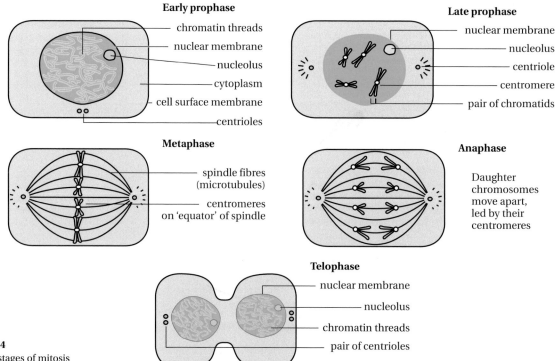

Early prophase
— chromatin threads
— nuclear membrane
— nucleolus
— cytoplasm
— cell surface membrane
— centrioles

Late prophase
— nuclear membrane
— nucleolus
— centriole
— centromere
— pair of chromatids

Metaphase
— spindle fibres (microtubules)
— centromeres on 'equator' of spindle

Anaphase
Daughter chromosomes move apart, led by their centromeres

Telophase
— nuclear membrane
— nucleolus
— chromatin threads
— pair of centrioles

Fig 24
The stages of mitosis

Interphase has three distinct phases:

- **G1 (growth phase 1)** New organelles are made and the volume of cytoplasm increases. If the cell is not going to divide, it will stay in the G1 phase, carrying out its normal functions. Immediately after mitosis the daughter cells are small, with a relatively large nucleus. As the cell matures the volume of cytoplasm increases until the cell reaches full size. When the cell is ready to divide again, it goes into the next two phases of interphase.

- **S (synthesis phase)** DNA is replicated.

- **G2 (growth phase 2)** The cell makes specific enzymes and other proteins needed to complete mitosis.

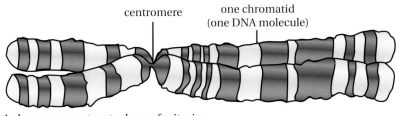

centromere

one chromatid
(one DNA molecule)

A chromosome at metaphase of mitosis

Fig 25
At the start of cell division, chromosomes appear as double structures consisting of two identical chromatids joined at the centromere. At anaphase, the paired chromosomes are pulled apart so each chromatid becomes a single chromosome. Note that the bands on the chromosomes in this diagram do *not* show individual genes

A chromosome at anaphase of mitosis, after the chromatids have separated

Cancer – mitosis out of control

Cells in the human body usually only divide when they should, in order to allow growth or the repair of tissues. At any one time, most cells are not dividing, they are in interphase. When the mechanisms that control the cell cycle break down, the result is the uncontrolled division, resulting in a swelling or growth known as a **tumour** (Fig 26).

There are two basic types of tumour:

- **Benign** tumours are enclosed in a capsule and grow in the centre; they don't invade the surrounding tissues. They are therefore not cancerous, and are often easily removed by surgery.

- **Malignant** tumours grow at the edges, invading the surrounding tissues and **organs**; they are cancerous, and are much more difficult to treat. Often it is difficult to tell where the boundaries of a malignant tumour are, making surgery difficult. Cells may break off and set up secondary tumours elsewhere in the body – this spreading process is called **metastasis** (Fig 26).

Many factors are involved in the development of cancer, including genetic and environmental factors.

Genetic factors and cancer

The development of cancer can be caused by a mutation in the genes that control cell division. Scientists have isolated several genes – **oncogenes** – whose mutation leads to the cell losing its ability to control cell division.

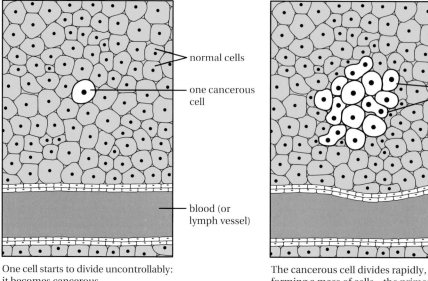

normal cells

one cancerous cell

rapidly dividing cancerous cells

blood (or lymph vessel)

One cell starts to divide uncontrollably: it becomes cancerous

The cancerous cell divides rapidly, forming a mass of cells – the primary tumour – which squashes out the neighbouring normal cells

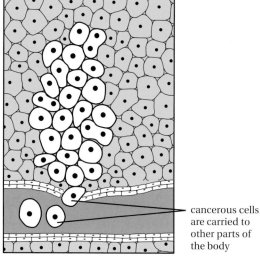

The process of metastasis. A clump of cells breaks free from the primary tumour and is then carried by the blood or lymphatic system to another part of the body. Fortunately, very few of these clumps of cells, about one in 10 000, are able to establish themselves and form a secondary tumour, but that is enough. Nearly 60% of people who are diagnosed with cancer are found to have well-established secondary tumours.

cancerous cells are carried to other parts of the body

Fig 26
The development of a tumour and the process of metastasis

However, the rate at which oncogenes mutate is much higher than the rate at which cancer occurs. Many malignant tumours are prevented by a back-up control system in the cell. **Tumour suppressor genes** stop cells dividing too quickly, giving time for the immune system to destroy the rogue cells, or for the damaged DNA to be repaired. If the tumour suppressor genes mutate, the cell's safety mechanisms are lost, and the development of cancer is more likely.

Cancer is more common in older people because their **somatic cells** (body cells) accumulate mutations. Sometimes, however, these mutations occur in gametes (sex cells), so that the mutated genes are passed on to the next generation. People who inherit these genes are said to have a **genetic predisposition** to cancer. This means they are more likely to develop cancer, especially at an early age.

Environmental factors

Exposure to many environmental factors increases the rate at which potentially cancerous mutations occur in cells (see above), and so increases the risk of developing cancer. These factors are called **carcinogens**.

Environmental factors known to lead to an increased risk of cancer include:

- **Smoking** – tobacco smoke contains a variety of carcinogens.

- **Diet** – several substances we eat or drink can cause cancer. For example, alcohol has been linked with a higher incidence of mouth, throat and oesophageal cancer. A lack of fibre and a high intake of red meat and animal fat seems to be associated with cancer of the colon and rectum, which is very common in the developed world.

- **Radiation** – certain types of radiation are known to be carcinogenic because they damage DNA. Ultra-violet radiation (in sunlight) does not penetrate far into human tissue, but it can cause skin cancer. Ionising radiation, for example from nuclear fallout, can penetrate much further and can cause cancers such as leukaemia (cancer of the bone marrow).

- **Chemical carcinogens** – asbestos, benzene, methanal (formaldehyde) and diesel exhaust fumes are all carcinogenic.

- **Some microorganisms** – notably viruses – have been linked with the development of cancers. The **human papilloma virus** is associated with over 90% of cases of **cervical cancer.**

Treatment of cancer

Broadly speaking, there are three treatments for cancer; surgery, chemotherapy and radiotherapy.

- **Surgery** involves cutting out the tumour – simple in principle, but some tumours can be very difficult to cut out. They may be located in a vital organ, or near vital blood vessels or nerves. It is also sometimes difficult to tell where the margins of the tumour are. This creates the double problem of needing to remove the entire tumour while preserving the healthy tissue.

- **Radiotherapy** involves treating the tumour with high doses of radiation, usually X-rays. High doses of radiation kill cells. The radiation can be focused on the tumour from an external source (an X-ray machine), or by placing radioactive material in or next to the tumour.

- **Chemotherapy** involves the injection of drugs that travel to all parts of the body. An ideal anti-cancer drug will target the tumour cells while leaving normal body cells unharmed, but this is not easy. Mitosis in the tumour is more rapid than in other tissues, and many anti-cancer drugs interfere with mitosis in some way. This also leads to damage in other areas of rapid mitosis such as bone marrow, skin and gut lining, but these normal cells usually recover once treatment is over.

Essential Notes

It seems odd that radiation can cause cancer, and radiation can be used to cure cancer. In small doses radiation damages DNA and causes mutations that can lead to cancer. The cells do not die. However, larger doses kill cells outright. When used in a highly directed beam, large doses can kill cancer cells in tumours, but not affect most of the healthy cells nearby.

3.2.6 In complex multicellular organisms, cells are organised into tissues, tissues into organs and organs into systems

We all start our life as a single fertilised egg, a **zygote**, which then divides by mitosis.

In early embryos the cells are unspecialised, but have the potential to **differentiate** into any of the 200 or so specialised cell types that make up the human body. These embryonic cells are the ultimate **stem cells**. They are known as **totipotent** because they have the power to turn into any other cell type.

Each body cell has a full set of genes, so the key to differentiation is the **selective activation** of genes – different genes are active in different cells. The tissues and organs of the body develop because cells differentiate in the right way at the right time.

- A **tissue** is an aggregation of similar cells. The human body is made up of four basic tissue types; nerve, muscle, connective and epithelial. Within these groups there are many sub-divisions.

- **Organs** are aggregations of tissues performing specific physiological functions. For example heart, liver, kidney.

- **Systems** are groups of organs that work together to achieve a major physiological function. Examples include digestive, respiratory, nervous and circulatory.

3.2.7 Factors such as size and metabolic rate affect the requirements of organisms and this gives rise to adaptations such as specialised exchange surfaces and mass transport systems

The size and surface area problem

All organisms need to exchange materials with their surroundings. They need to exchange respiratory gases (carbon dioxide and oxygen), take in food and get rid of waste. The quantity of materials that an organism *needs* to exchange varies according to its *volume* – the amount of living tissue it has.

However, the quantity of a particular material that an organism is *able to exchange* is proportional to its surface area. *As organisms get larger, the surface area : volume ratio decreases.* (See Table 1). For larger organisms, this effect is a problem. It makes it increasingly difficult to exchange both materials and heat with the environment fast enough to keep conditions inside the organism constant.

Table 1
Surface area and volume of a cube

Length of side/mm	Surface area/mm^2	Volume/mm^3	Surface area : volume ratio
1	6	1	6
2	24	8	3
3	54	27	2
10	600	1000	0.6

Surface area, heat and metabolic rate

The control of body temperature is known as **thermoregulation**. Mammals and birds can maintain a constant core body temperature using their physiology and their behaviour. They are said to be **endothermic** because their body heat is generated inside the body.

All other animals are, to a large extent, at the mercy of the environment. They can gain or lose heat by their behaviour, for example, crocodiles gape to keep cool, and many reptiles bask in the sun to warm up. However, their body temperature generally reflects that of their surroundings. These organisms are said to be **ectothermic** because their body heat comes mainly from outside their body.

Mammals and birds produce heat as a by-product of metabolism, and thermoregulate by controlling its loss into the environment. The amount of heat an organism can make depends on two things:

- Its volume, in other words, the mass of living tissue that it has
- Its **metabolic rate**, the number and speed of chemical reactions going on in its cells.

Metabolic rate can be measured by the amount of oxygen the animal uses (volume of oxygen per unit body weight per unit time) or by the amount of heat it produces (kJ of energy per unit body weight per unit time).

A large animal, such as an elephant or a hippopotamus, has a huge amount of heat-producing tissue and a relatively small surface area through which to lose it. Such an animal needs strategies to lose heat. These can include:

- Physical adaptations – large ears with a good blood supply near to the surface, to lose heat from the blood
- Behavioural adaptations – increasing evaporation of water from the body surface by mud and water bathing
- Physiological adaptations – having a relatively low metabolic rate.

Small animals, such as shrews, have the opposite problem. Their surface area to volume ratio is so large that the animal must have a very high metabolic rate to keep warm. Shrews have to eat constantly so that they have enough fuel to respire and generate body heat.

Why do organisms need to exchange gases?

There are three main reasons:

- Most organisms take in oxygen and release carbon dioxide during aerobic respiration
- In anaerobic conditions, some organisms, such as yeast and bacteria, release carbon dioxide without absorbing oxygen
- Plants take in carbon dioxide and release oxygen when photosynthesis exceeds the rate of aerobic respiration.

Gas exchange occurs by diffusion, and gas exchange organs all show the same basic adaptations that maximise diffusion:

- a large surface area
- thin membranes, so the distance for diffusion is as short as possible
- an efficient transport system.

Examiners' Notes

A common mistake is to say that a large animal has a small surface area. An elephant has a very large surface area, but it has a small *surface area to volume ratio*.

Gas exchange in single-celled organisms

Single-celled organisms include bacteria and several different types of protoctist, including algae and amoeba. Being small, they have a large surface area to volume ratio, so the exchange of materials is no problem. Exchange takes place over the whole surface of the organism. However, for organisms to become larger (more than about 1 mm³) they must become multicellular, and have some way of increasing the surface area for exchange of materials and heat.

Some multicellular organisms are elongated, flat or hollow, such as sea anemones and tapeworms, which are both invertebrates. In these organisms, materials exchanged between the cells and the environment have only a short distance to diffuse.

More complex multicellular organisms have evolved specialist gas exchange organs such as lungs, which are covered in Unit 1. Three more gas exchange solutions are studied here: gas exchange in insects, fish and plants.

Gas exchange in insects

Insects solve the gas exchange problem in a unique way. They have a **tracheal system** that consists of a network of tubes that branch out and take air directly from the outside and into the respiring tissues (Fig 27).

Fig 27
The tracheal system in insects. Air enters tiny tracheoles that pass very close to each respiring cell. The distances involved are so short that diffusion is rapid and efficient enough to meet the insect's needs

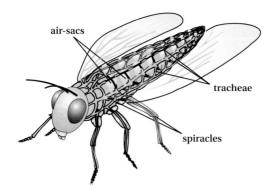
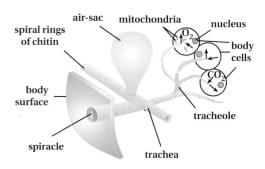

Air enters through holes in the insect's exoskeleton called **spiracles**. It then passes into tubes called **tracheae** (sing. trachea), which branch out into smaller **tracheoles**. The key difference between these two types of tube is that tracheae have thicker supportive walls whereas tracheoles have thin permeable walls that allow gas exchange.

The tracheoles form a fine network of tubes that pass within a short diffusing distance of all the respiring cells in the insect's body. Some tracheoles actually enter the cells, delivering oxygen directly to the mitochondria.

Essential Notes

Compared to the animal system, this may seem to be a strange way to breathe air, but diffusion of O_2 and CO_2 through air is very rapid, making gas exchange highly efficient.

Insects can open or close their spiracles to alter the level of ventilation, and to minimise water loss. Some insects with a high metabolic rate are able to increase ventilation by contracting the muscles of their abdomen.

Gas exchange in fish

The gills of a fish are adapted for gas exchange in water, which is much denser than air but contains less available oxygen making it harder to extract a large volume of oxygen from water than from air. Animals that breathe in water are all cold blooded ectotherms and have a lower oxygen demand than mammals or birds.

Air versus water as a breathing medium

Air and water have very different properties and require completely different gas exchange systems:

- Air contains about 20% oxygen compared with around 1% or less for water.

- The oxygen content of air is very stable, whereas the oxygen content of water can vary considerably. The warmer the water, the lower the amount of dissolved oxygen it can hold.

- Diffusion of gases is much faster through air than through water. As a consequence, diffusion is rapid through the tracheoles of insects and the air sacs of mammalian lungs. However, it is slow where it has to pass through the liquid lining the alveoli and, of course, in fish gills.

- Water is much denser than air, so it takes much more effort to move it around. Air-breathing animals can inhale, reverse the direction of flow and breathe out with comparatively little effort. It would not be possible to do this with large volumes of water, so aquatic organisms let water flow over their gills in one direction only.

Gas exchange in the fish gill

The essential gas exchange features of a gill are:

- The **gill lamellae** and **gill filaments** have a large surface area (Fig 28).
- The **countercurrent system** facilitates gas exchange (Fig 29).

The numerous gill filaments, and even more numerous lamellae, have a rich blood supply. Their thin membranes allow blood to come very close to the water. The blood in the capillaries flows in the opposite direction to the way water flows over the gills, which is why this is known as a countercurrent system.

If the blood and water flowed in the same direction, oxygen would diffuse into the blood until an equilibrium was reached, at which point there would be no further net gas exchange. At any point along the filament in a countercurrent system, the blood always has a lower concentration of oxygen than the water next to it (see Fig 29). So, a diffusion gradient is maintained along the entire length of the filament. This ensures that oxygen can diffuse into the blood at every point along the filament and that the blood leaving the filament has a high concentration of oxygen.

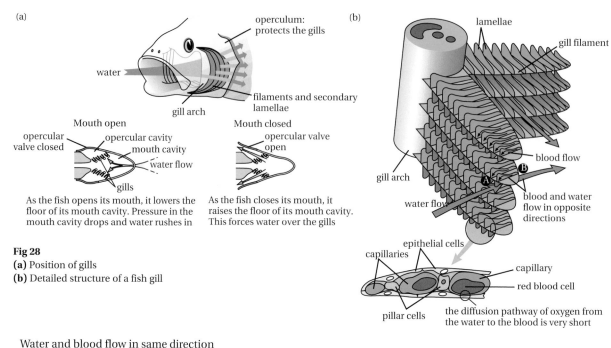

Fig 28
(a) Position of gills
(b) Detailed structure of a fish gill

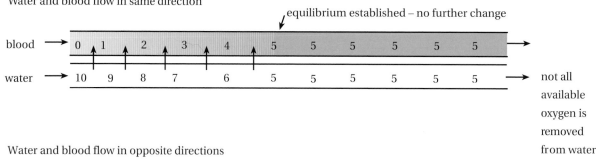

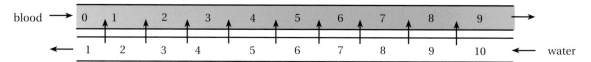

Fig 29
Diagram showing the importance of the countercurrent system. The numbers refer to relative concentrations of dissolved oxygen. When blood flows in the opposite direction to the water, it continues to pass water that contains a higher concentration of oxygen. Thus the countercurrent system allows the blood to absorb much more oxygen

Gas exchange in plants

The leaf is an organ adapted to maximise photosynthesis. As photosynthesis requires carbon dioxide and produces oxygen, the leaf must be an efficient gas exchange structure. The palisade cells carry out most of the photosynthesis, and so the structure of the leaf centres around giving the palisade cells what they need (light, carbon dioxide and water) and taking away what they produce (sugar and oxygen). A section through the leaf (Fig 30) shows the follow1ing adaptations:

- Loosely packed mesophyll cells. This means there are air spaces between cells, providing a large surface area for gas exchange.

- **Stomata** open to allow gases to diffuse in and out of the internal air spaces along their concentration gradients (the stomata close at night to reduce water loss).

These adaptations mean that the cells that carry out the most photosynthesis are in direct contact with the environment.

Essential Notes

The syllabus specifies a dicotyledonous plant, or dicot, which generally means a 'standard' flowering plant. There are two main types of flowering plants: the monocotyledons, for example, the grasses, and the **dicotyledons**, which include most other familiar flowering plant species.

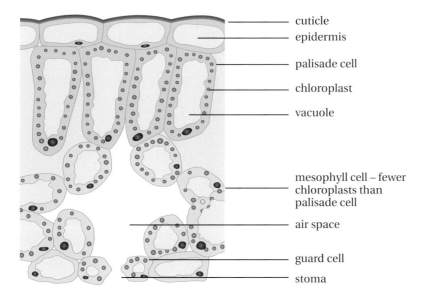

cuticle
epidermis
palisade cell
chloroplast
vacuole

mesophyll cell – fewer chloroplasts than palisade cell

air space

guard cell

stoma

Fig 30
A section through the leaf of a dicotyledonous plant

Mass transport

There are many different organs of gas exchange such as lungs and gills, but these organs would be ineffective without a distribution network to the rest of the body. To be effective, gas exchange organs need a circulatory system, which usually takes the form of a network of tubes or vessels that connects to all parts of the organism.

Many organisms have vascular systems (vascular = tube/vessel). Plants have xylem and phloem while many animals have a circulatory blood system. The movement of large volumes of fluid and dissolved substances within a transport system is known as **mass flow**.

The mammalian blood system

Mammals are endothermic animals with a high metabolic rate and so they need an efficient circulatory system to deliver large amounts of food and oxygen to the living cells, and to take away the rapidly accumulating wastes. To achieve this, mammals have a double circulation; a **pulmonary circulation** and a **systemic circulation**.

The pulmonary circulation takes blood on the relatively short journey from the heart to the lungs, where blood is oxygenated. When blood passes through a system of capillaries *it loses pressure*, so it must return to the heart for a pressure boost before it enters the systemic circulation, which takes blood around the rest of the body.

(a)

(b)

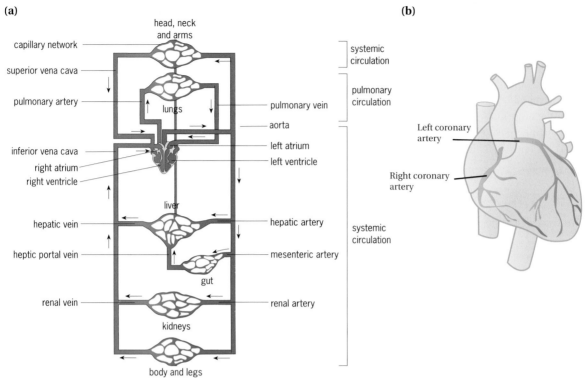

Fig 31
(a) The major blood vessels
(b) The coronary arteries supply blood
to the heart muscle itself

Blood vessels

The structure and function of arteries, arterioles, veins and capillaries are summarised in Table 2 and their interrelationship is shown in Fig 32.

Fig 32
An overview of the different types of blood vessels

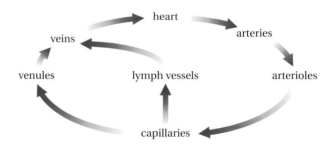

Capillaries and tissue fluid

Tissue fluid surrounds all living cells. Cells obtain all their oxygen and nutrients from this fluid, swapping them for carbon dioxide and other wastes, such as area. Its composition is similar to blood plasma, but without the large proteins. The function of capillaries is to allow the exchange of materials between tissue fluid and the blood (Fig 33).

Keeping the composition of tissue fluid constant is a major aspect of **homeostasis**. To understand how this is achieved we need to know two things:

● Why does tissue fluid form?

● Why does it drain away?

Vessel	Diagram	Structure of wall	Function
Artery		Contains more elastic fibres than muscle; tough walls can withstand pressure surges as the heart beats	Recoil; absorbs pressure when heart beats. Smooths out pulse wave. Maintains diastolic blood pressure
Arteriole		Contains more muscle than elastic fibres; can **constrict** or **dilate**	control blood supply to particular areas
Capillary	endothelial cell	thin, permeable	allow rapid diffusion and exchange
Vein		relatively thin; contain valves	prevent backflow

Table 2
Relating structure to function in blood vessel walls

Two forces are important:

- **Hydrostatic pressure** – the fluid pressure of the blood, created by the left ventricle of the heart. This forces fluid out of the blood and into the tissues, forming tissue fluid.

- **Water potential** – this force, generated mainly by the proteins in the plasma, tends to draw fluid back into the blood by osmosis, which is why tissue fluid can drain away.

Fig 33
Capillaries are found in between all the living cells of the body, allowing blood to flow there, bringing materials to replenish tissue fluid and taking away the waste

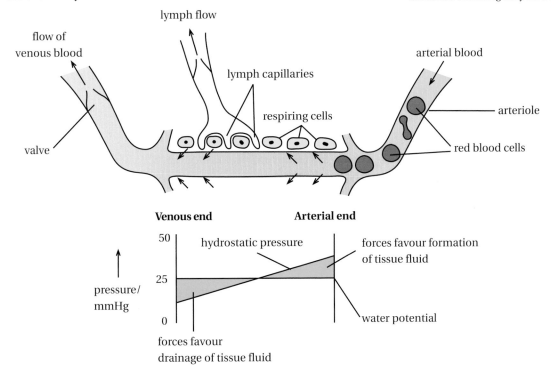

Tissue fluid is formed at the arterial end of a capillary because the hydrostatic pressure is greater than the water potential force. However, as fluid passes along the capillary it loses volume and, therefore, its pressure drops. When the hydrostatic pressure falls below the water potential, fluid drains back into the blood.

Arteries deliver all of the fluid to the tissues, but the veins do not drain all of it away. The lymphatic system drains away a small but vital proportion of tissue fluid. This fluid passes into progressively larger **lymph** vessels, before draining into the blood system in the upper part of the chest cavity.

Plants and water

Plants can make their own food and, so, are fundamentally different from animals, which have to go and search for it. It should be no surprise that plants don't need muscles or a moveable skeleton.

Plants range in complexity from the simplest mosses and liverworts, through ferns and conifers, to the flowering plants. You have to know about the largest group of flowering plants, the dicotyledons (dicots for short). Most dicots are land-living plants and have specialised structures as shown in Fig 34. These include leaves, flowers, fruits and seeds, all supported by roots and a stem:

- **Leaves** are usually adapted to maximise the process of photosynthesis, although some plants, such as cacti, use their leaves for other purposes, such as defence.
- **Roots** are adapted to absorb nutrients (*not food!*) from the soil or water. Roots also anchor the plant and may be important organs for storage and/or **perennation** (surviving from one year to the next).
- **Flowers** are organs of sexual reproduction.

Root structure

Fig 34b shows the basic structure of a root. The following root tissues are of key importance:

- **Endodermis** – literally, the 'inner skin'. This is a thin layer of cells that surrounds the **vascular** (conducting) **tissue**. The endodermis contains a waterproof layer, the **Casparian strip** that allows the plant to control the movement of ions into the xylem.
- **Root hair cells**– these are elongated **epidermal** (outer skin) cells that project into the soil. Root hairs greatly increase the surface area of the root, allowing it to absorb more water and minerals.
- **Xylem** – this tissue consists of many dead, hollow xylem vessels that carry water and dissolved mineral ions up the plant to the leaves and other organs.
- **Phloem** – this is tissue consisting mainly of living cells, which are tubular in shape. These cells are responsible for **translocation** in which dissolved organic materials, such as sucrose, are moved around the plant.

Water uptake and the transpiration stream

You need to know two vital definitions:

Transpiration is the loss of water from the surfaces of a plant that are above the ground. Most water is lost through the stomata on the underside of leaves.

The **transpiration stream** is the continuous flow of water through the plant, from the roots to the leaves. The xylem tissue is mainly responsible for this flow.

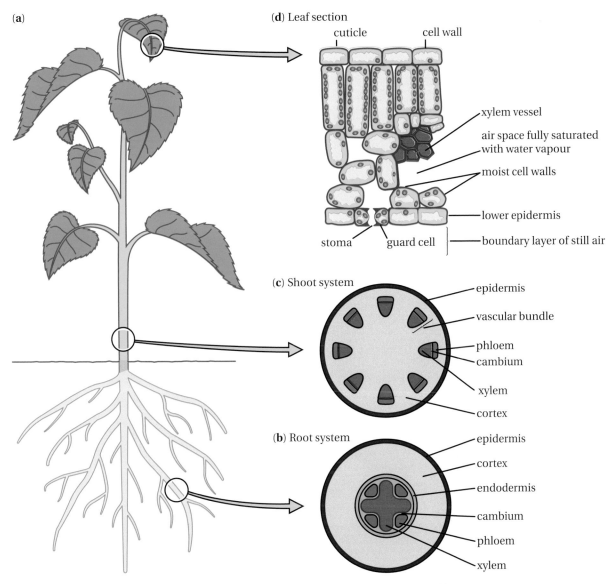

(a)

(d) Leaf section
- cuticle
- cell wall
- xylem vessel
- air space fully saturated with water vapour
- moist cell walls
- lower epidermis
- boundary layer of still air
- stoma
- guard cell

(c) Shoot system
- epidermis
- vascular bundle
- phloem
- cambium
- xylem
- cortex

(b) Root system
- epidermis
- cortex
- endodermis
- cambium
- phloem
- xylem

Fig 34
(a) Basic structure of a dicot
(b) Section through a root. Note the central vascular bundle and the x-shaped xylem
(c) Section through a stem. Note the separate vascular bundles
(d) Section through a leaf

Uptake of water by the roots

Fig 35 shows the pathway taken by water from soil to the xylem in the centre of the root. Water enters the root because the water potential of the soil water is less negative (in other words greater) than that of the cell sap, so water enters by osmosis. As water enters the first cell it raises the cell's water potential above that of the next cell, so water passes from cell to cell towards the centre of the root. Water is pulled continuously up the xylem vessels and out through the leaves into the atmosphere. Throughout its journey up the plant, water moves down a water potential gradient (Fig 36).

Water can take two different pathways through the tissues of a plant:

- Through the living tissue, through the cytoplasm of cells. This is the **symplast** pathway. About 10% of water moves this way.

- Through the non-living tissue, in-between the cell walls and spaces around cells. This is the **apoplast pathway**. About 90% of water takes this route.

Fig 35
The apoplast and symplast pathways are the two major routes from the soil to the xylem in the centre of the root. The Casparian strip diverts the apolpast pathway, forcing it to switch to the symplast pathway at that point

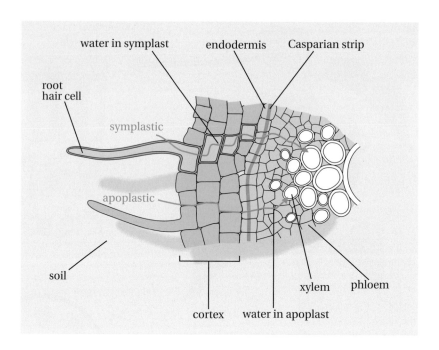

Fig 36
Water passes through the plant along a water potential gradient. The water potential is least negative in the soil water and most negative in the atmosphere

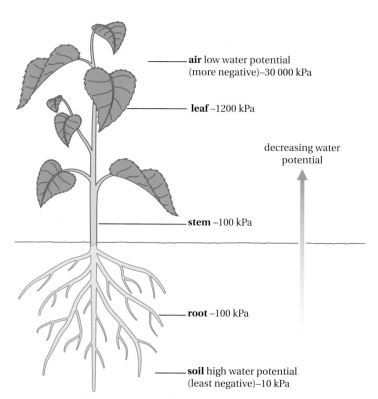

water potential of the soil solution is high (close to zero) because the soil solution is a very dilute solution of ions

Before water and minerals can pass into the xylem, they must pass through the endodermis, the thin membrane that surrounds the vascular tissue. A waterproof layer, the Casparian strip, lies between the endodermal cells and the vascular bundle, blocking the apoplast pathway. This is significant because the plant has control of what passes through the cytoplasm (and so has control over materials in the symplast pathway) but cannot control the movement of substances through the spaces in between cells.

The Casparian strip allows the cells to control the movement of ions into the xylem. The Casparian strip blocks the apoplast pathway, so water and ions have to pass through the symplast pathway, which has living membranes and cytoplasm, with their selective permeability and active transport mechanisms. This gives the plant some control over ion flow into the xylem.

Without the Casparian strip and the symplast pathway, the plant would just act as a wick, drawing up large amounts of water and mineral ions from the soil to the leaves. As the water evaporated, the ion concentration would continually build up, eventually damaging the plant tissue.

Is water pushed or pulled up a plant?

The simple answer is; a bit of both. Two forces act to move water upwards:

- **Root pressure**, which pushes water up from beneath
- **Cohesion tension**, which draws water down from above.

Watching what happens when a stem is cut can demonstrate which is more important. If root pressure was greater, there would be a *positive* pressure in the stem – fluid would flow out of a cut stem. This sometimes happens, especially in small and younger plants, but usually there is a *negative* pressure inside the vessels of the stem showing that water is *pulled* up the plant. If a stem under negative pressure is cut, air is drawn in rather than fluid spurting out.

Root pressure

Root pressure arises because mineral ions are actively taken up into the xylem in the root. If there is no transpiration, or it is very slow, these ions are not transported up the stem, they build up in the root xylem. This lowers the water potential in the root tissue and water is drawn into the root by osmosis. Water continually enters the xylem and pushes a column of water upwards. Root pressure is important in young plants as it achieves water transport before the leaves of young seedlings are big enough for cohesion tension to be great enough to pull water up the stem.

The cohesion-tension hypothesis

The main driving force of transpiration, which *pulls* water up the plant, is known as the cohesion–tension hypothesis. As water evaporates from the leaves, it creates a negative pressure in the xylem. This pulls a continuous column of water up from the roots. Water molecules are very cohesive; they stick together, forming a column with great tensile strength from the surface of the mesophyll cells (Fig 37), down the xylem to the roots.

The factors that raise the rate of transpiration are those that increase evaporation:

- **Temperature** – the higher the temperature, the faster water molecules evaporate
- **Humidity** – the amount of water vapour in the air. The more humid it is, the harder it is for water vapour to move out of the air spaces. The drier it is, the greater the **water potential gradient** between the air spaces and the atmosphere.

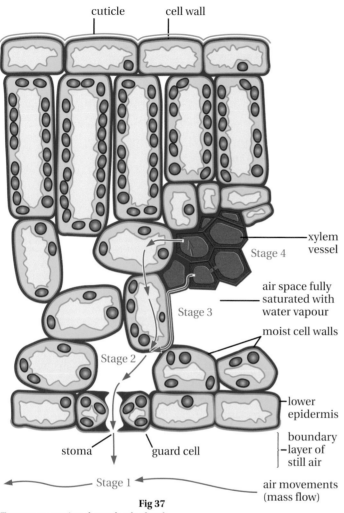

cuticle   cell wall

xylem vessel

Stage 4

air space fully saturated with water vapour

Stage 3

moist cell walls

Stage 2

lower epidermis

boundary layer of still air

stoma   guard cell

Stage 1

air movements (mass flow)

Fig 37
Transverse section through a leaf and the flow of water vapour

Stage 1. Mass flow in air

Wind movements (mass flow) take air, fully saturated with water vapour, away from the leaf surface.

The air replacing it contains less water vapour and this maintains a concentration gradient for water vapour leaving the air spaces of a leaf.

Stage 2. Diffusion of water in still air

Water vapour diffuses down a concentration gradient through the leaf air spaces, through open stomata, and through the boundary layer of still air on the outside of the leaf.

Stage 3. Diffusion of water through cells

Water loss from the surface of cells lowers the water potential inside the cells.

Water at a higher potential diffuses from the nearest xylem vessel through leaf cells to replace the lost water.

Stage 4. Mass flow of water in xylem vessels

Pressure in xylem vessels is lowered as water leaves them.

Water moves up the xylem vessel from the roots where the pressure is higher.

- **Air movement** – for example, wind speed. A breeze blows away the small pockets of humid air that develop around stomata when the air is still; humid air is replaced by drier air, so the water potential gradient is maintained.

- **Light** – this causes stomata to open, greatly increasing the passage of water vapour out of the plant.

Essential Notes

The circumference of a tree shows a measurable decrease when the plant is actively transpiring. The pull on the column of water actually makes the xylem vessels narrower. If the xylem vessels are pierced by a needle, however, air is drawn in, breaking the column and blocking the transpiration stream.

Examiners' Notes

The conditions that increase the speed of drying of clothes on a washing line – warm, dry, windy – also speed up transpiration.

Measuring transpiration – the potometer

The **potometer** is a simple device for measuring the rate of transpiration from a cutting (Fig 38). Think of the glass tube as a transparent extension of the xylem.

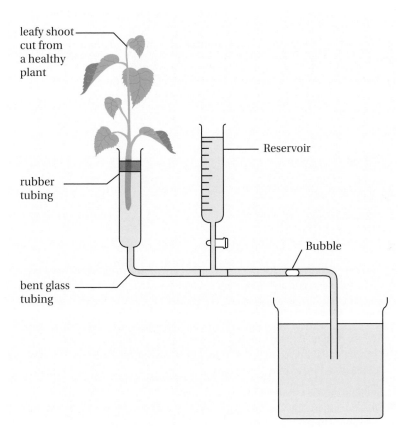

leafy shoot cut from a healthy plant

rubber tubing

bent glass tubing

Reservoir

Bubble

Fig 38
A potometer is a useful piece of apparatus for measuring the rate of transpiration from a cutting

How it works:

- The shoot transpires
- This results in water being drawn up the xylem
- The bubble in the tube shows the rate of water uptake
- The speed that the bubble moves is a measure of the rate of transpiration.

You can measure the volume of water being transpired in two ways:

1 By having the bubble in a calibrated tube of known volume.

2 By having a calibrated reservoir, and measuring the volume needed to move the bubble back to the start. This also allows the potometer to be re-started without having to dismantle all the apparatus.

The potometer can be used to measure the effect of various environmental conditions on the rate of transpiration. Light intensity, wind speed, relative humidity and temperature can all be investigated.

In practice, it is difficult to control all the variables. In particular, in order to get reliable data it is necessary to repeat the experiment using different shoots, and it is near impossible to get identical ones. They will differ in a variety of important ways, number and size of leaves, thickness of xylem tissue, number of stomata, water content of cells etc.

To compensate for the difference between shoots, it is necessary to calculate the surface area of each one. This is done by removing the leaves after the experiment and estimating their surface area by using squared paper. The units of transpiration are usually **water loss per unit area per minute**; $cm^3 H_2O/m^2/min$.

Table 3 shows sample results from an investigation into the effect of air movement. For each trial, the water loss was measured every two minutes for 20 minutes

Table 3
Sample results obtained using a potometer. Note that reading 4 has not been used in calculating the average for still air as it is an anomalous reading. While almost all biological data varies, an anamalous result is one that falls outside the normal range.

Trial number	Water loss $cm^3 H_2O/m^2/min$					
	1	2	3	4	5	Average
Still air	2.4	2.8	3.1	0.6	2.5	2.7
Moving air	6.2	5.6	6.0	5.6	4.9	5.66

In order to get **valid** results the data needs to be **accurate**, **precise** and **reliable**:

- Accurate results are close to the true value. Possible problems that will make the results inaccurate include a leaky seal between the shoot and the tube, incorrectly calibrated glassware or perhaps a fracture/break in the xylem tissue.

- Precise results depend on the nature of the apparatus being used. With a potometer calibrated in 0.1 ml intervals, it is plainly silly to have readings of 5.3428. Reading to one decimal place is precise enough in this situation.

- Reliable data is obtained by doing repeats, so that all of the readings are close together. Any anomalous results, such as the 0.6 reading in trial 4, should not be included in the calculation of the mean.

The conclusion from these results, of course, is that plants transpire faster in windy conditions.

3.2.8 Classification is a means of organising the variety of life based on relationships between organisms and is built round the concept of species

There are, at present, over two million different species that have been discovered and therefore given a **scientific name**. Many more are yet to be classified.

The science of classification is known as **taxonomy**, and it aims to produce a catalogue of all living things on Earth, and as complete a picture of evolution as possible. This is not easy. This is one area of science where there is very little agreement. Systems and ideas are constantly changing as new evidence comes to light.

To set the scene:

- The Earth is very old – 4,600,000,000 (4.6 billion) years old is our current best estimate

- Life probably evolved about 3.5 billion years ago

- The extinct species greatly outnumber the living ones

- Most species, especially the soft-bodied ones, did not leave fossils

- Organisms did not evolve according to neat patterns and systems for the convenience of scientists

- New evidence is coming to light all the time. Modern techniques of DNA and protein analysis (see next section) throw new light on evolutionary relationships, so that our ideas about what evolved from what, and what is related to what, are constantly changing.

Scientific names

All species are given a scientific name, which usually comes from Latin or Greek. This name is used across all language barriers, and avoids confusion when referring to a particular species.

Scientific names are **binomial** – they have two parts. The first part, the **generic name**, is the name of the **genus** and has a capital letter. The **specific name** follows, and does not have a capital letter. For example, *Canis familiaris* is the domestic dog, while *Gorilla gorilla* is, (unsurprisingly), the gorilla. Scientific names should be given in italics or underlined.

This is described as a **phylogenetic** system of classification – it is one based on evolutionary history. It's a bit like a family tree that goes back millions of years. To construct a phylogenetic tree, scientists use anatomical/physical features, fossil records and, increasingly, biochemical analysis of DNA and proteins (see below).

The taxonomy uses a layered structure or **hierarchy**, one version of which is shown in Table 4. Its key features are:

- It consists of a series of groups within groups, from the most general (kingdom) to the most specific (species).

- There is no overlap between the groups. For instance, there is no organism that is part amphibian and part reptile – it is either in one group or the other.

- The groups are based on shared features. The more specific the group, the more shared features there are.

Examiners' Notes

It may help to invent a mnemonic to remember the sequence of kingdom, phylum etc. Make up a phrase according to KPCOFGS, such as Keep Putting Cabbages On Fat Greasy Slugs, or something more memorable/silly/personal to you.

Taxon	Humans as an example	Explanation
Kingdom	Animalia	We are animals – see the five kingdoms explanation below
Phylum	Chordates	We possess a backbone
Class	Mammals	We have warm blood, fur and feed our young on milk
Order	Primates	We have large brains, grasping hands, fingernails, binocular colour vision
Family	Hominids	Man-like creatures, only one species not extinct
Genus	*Homo*	Literally 'man'
Species	*sapiens*	Literally 'thinking'

Table 4
Taxonomic hierarchy. Many groups of organism do not fall neatly into these seven categories, hence the need for additional categories such as suborder and infraclass.

What is a species?

A useful working definition of a species is:

A group of individuals that have observable similarities and the ability to interbreed and produce fertile offspring.

This definition works well enough for most situations, including A-level examinations. Lions and tigers can mate to produce ligers or tigons, while horses and donkeys can produce mules, but in all cases the hybrid offspring are infertile.

However, there are problems with this definition. Domestic dogs, wolves and coyotes can all interbreed to produce perfectly fertile offspring, and there are many other examples. The problem lies partly in the process of speciation, which can take time, and partly from our desire to give things precise definitions.

A better definition of a species is therefore:

A group of organisms that have similar physical, behavioural and biochemical features, that can interbreed to produce fertile offspring, and that do not normally interbreed with any other group of organisms.

The overall organisation – nobody can agree!

Classification is a good example of how science works. Ideas and models are constantly being revised in the light of new evidence. For many years scientists have put organisms into two groups on the basis of their cellular organisation – the prokaryotes and the eukaryotes. Then some scientists argued that the prokaryotes should be split into two – the Eubacteria and Archaebacteria. At the moment there is some strong support for the idea that above the level of kingdom there are three **domains**, **Bacteria**, **Archaea** and **Eukarya**.

The five kingdoms

Some scientists have accepted a five-kingdom system of classification. All organisms can be placed into one of these five kingdoms. Four contain the eukaryotic organisms while a fifth contains the prokaryotes – the bacteria. Many other scientists feel that the prokaryotes should be split into two or more kingdoms. The four eukaryote kingdoms are Animals, Plants, Fungi and Protoctista.

3.2.9 Originally classification systems were based on observable features but more recent approaches draw on a wider range of evidence to clarify relationships between organisms

Scientists have long been attempting to construct phylogenetic trees in an attempt to clarify the history of life on Earth. Early attempts were based on shared features, mainly anatomical. All scientists had to work on were living or preserved specimens, and fossils. Phylogenetic trees were constructed using shared features such as body plan, skeletal structure, and so on. In the last two decades, however, molecular studies have moved us into a new era.

DNA and protein analysis

Every living organism contains DNA, RNA and proteins. Closely related organisms generally have a high degree of similarity in the sequences of bases or amino acids, whereas the molecules of distantly related organisms usually show fewer similarities. This is because mutations accumulate over time. **Molecular phylogeny** uses this data to build 'relationship trees' that show the probable evolution of various organisms (Fig 39).

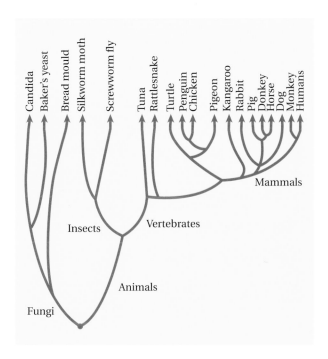

Fig 39
A phylogenetic tree based on the amino acid sequence data of cytochrome C. The relationship between the tuna, rattlesnake, turtle and three species of bird is surprising, and does not reflect the traditional view of things

DNA hybridisation

DNA hybridisation can be used to estimate the degree of similarity between two species, for example human and gorilla (Fig 40). The technique determines the genetic distance between two species. When several species are compared in this way, the similarity values allow the species to be arranged in a phylogenetic tree (Fig 39).

The basic process is as follows:

1   DNA samples are taken from two species, cut into short sequences and heated to about 90 $^{\circ}$C. This causes the DNA to denature: the hydrogen bonds break and the two strands come apart.

2   The DNA from the two species is mixed and then allowed to cool down.

3   Some strands of DNA re-join, some form hybrid DNA molecules with one strand from each of the two species.

Different strands of DNA have different melting points. This is because C≡G pairings are harder to break than A=T. The higher the percentage of C≡G in the sample, the higher the temperature at which it denatures.

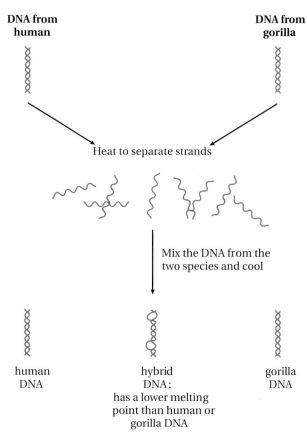

DNA from human

DNA from gorilla

Heat to separate strands

Mix the DNA from the two species and cool

human DNA

hybrid DNA: has a lower melting point than human or gorilla DNA

gorilla DNA

Fig 40
The technique of DNA hybridisation

The temperature at which the two strands **re-anneal** tells us about the degree of similarity between them:

- When two strands from the same species re-anneal, they do so at 87 °C. This is because they have many sequences in common and form hydrogen bonds along the length of the molecule.

- The hybrid DNA must cool to a lower temperature before it can re-anneal, because there are fewer matching base sequences and so fewer hydrogen bonds to hold them together.

Protein differences: what they can tell us about evolution

Proteins are made up of many amino acids, arranged in a specific sequence. The sequence of a particular protein is likely to be very similar in two closely related species, but may be different in two species that are separated by millions of years of evolution. So, comparing sequences in proteins that fulfil basic functions in the cell can tell us a lot about the path of evolution.

For example, scientists have looked at the protein **cytochrome c**, which is a protein that occurs on the surface of the inner membrane of the mitochondria. Because this protein is essential to the electron transfer reactions of respiration that take place there, it doesn't change very much over time. The only mutations that are possible are ones that do not affect its function.

Comparing cytochrome c sequences between species tells us whether they had a common ancestry, and how recently. For example, humans share exactly the same cytochrome c molecule with chimpanzees, but the protein in the rhesus monkey is different by one amino acid. A yeast has a cytochrome c that differs by 51 amino acids. Looking at the number of amino acid differences that exist between different species in different proteins can be used to construct very complex phylogenetic trees.

Courtship behaviour is a necessary precursor to successful mating

Courtship behaviour enables animals to achieve several things:

- To recognise and seek out a member of the same species
- To approach a potential mate safely and without aggression
- To choose a strong and healthy mate
- To form a pair bond and synchronise breeding behaviour.

Species recognition

This is important when closely related species are found together. Think of butterflies, birds, insects and frogs in a tropical rainforest. Strategies that ensure the same species mate include courtship displays and dances, mating calls and pheromones (chemical signals). Firefly species even have their own particular sequence of flashes.

Avoiding aggression

When not mating, most animals have an **individual space** that reduces the risk of aggression and also reduces the spread of disease. Courtship enables this space to be invaded without triggering aggression.

Choosing a strong and healthy mate

Breeding is a major investment of time and energy. Before mating, animals can improve their chances of reproductive success by selecting a mate that is fit and healthy. Some female birds, such as terns, test out the suitability of a potential mate by inviting him to feed her. If he can deliver plenty of fish, she will mate with him.

Forming a pair bond

There are many species that form pair bonds, because it is one strategy that increases the chances of survival of the offspring. All animals invest a lot of energy in reproduction. At one end of the scale is the salmon, which lays a huge number of eggs and promptly dies. At the other end of the scale are animals such as humans that have very few offspring but invest a lot of energy in parental care.

3.2.10 Adaptation and selection are major components of evolution and make a significant contribution to the diversity of living organisms

Antibiotics

Antibiotics are a large group of naturally occurring and synthesised drugs that combat bacterial infection. Antibiotics work by interfering with prokaryote metabolism but leave the eukaryotic cells of the host working normally. Basically, antibiotics work in one of three different ways:

- They prevent the formation of bacterial cell walls, leaving them liable to absorb water by osmosis, swell and burst

- They interfere with DNA replication
- They interfere with protein synthesis.

Bactericidal antibiotics kill the targeted microorganisms.

Bacteriostatic antibiotics prevent the targeted microorganisms from multiplying.

The bacteria fight back: antibiotic resistance

As soon as there was wide-scale use of antibiotics, bacteria began to fight back by developing resistance to them. Penicillin use began in 1942, and by 1947 there were reports of resistant strains that did not respond to treatment. Since then, antibiotic resistant bacteria – called **'superbugs'** by the media – have become big news and their emergence is a classic example of evolution in action.

There are three vital aspects to consider:

- How does resistance arise?
- How does resistance spread?
- What is the effect of human behaviour?

Understanding bacterial resistance required an understanding of the structure of a bacterium and its DNA (fig 41).

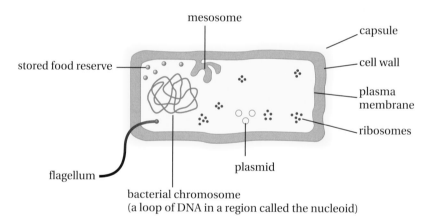

Fig 41
The genetic material in bacteria. There is one large chromosome made from circular DNA in an area called the nucleoid. This contains all the genes needed for vital life processes, such as respiration. There are also many tiny loops of DNA called plasmids. The proteins that plasmid genes code for are useful rather than essential, for example, antibiotic resistance genes

How does resistance arise?

Resistance develops when bacterial genes mutate, forming new alleles. Resistance alleles make proteins that in some way make the individual bacterium resist the killing action of an antibiotic. There are several possible modes of action:

- The protein breaks down the antibiotic
- The protein alters membrane permeability so the antibiotic cannot get into the bacterium, or is pumped out as quickly as it enters
- The protein provides an alternative metabolic pathway. If the antibiotic works in wild type bacteria by blocking a vital enzyme, resistance can develop if a mutated allele codes for a new enzyme that works in an alternative biochemical pathway.

How does resistance spread?

Antibiotic resistance spreads in two ways:

- **Vertical gene transmission** This involves passing the resistance allele from mother cell to daughter cells, and of course this happens within the same species of bacterium.

- **Horizontal gene transmission** This involves passing resistance alleles from one species to another, and is common in bacteria (Fig 42).

Genetic material can be transferred from one individual to another by the process of **conjugation**. Most conjugation occurs between bacteria of the same species, but this is not always the case. So antibiotic resistance can arise in one species, and the allele can be passed on to another, perhaps more pathogenic species.

Examiners' Notes

A common mistake is to imply that the bacteria 'decide' to become resistant. The resistance alleles are already present in some fortunate individuals, or a very timely mutation produces a resistance allele *by chance.*

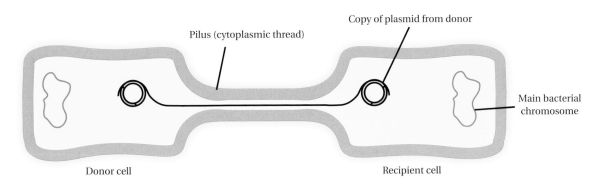

Pilus (cytoplasmic thread)

Copy of plasmid from donor

Main bacterial chromosome

Donor cell

Recipient cell

Fig 42
Bacterial conjugation is the transfer of genetic material between two bacteria in direct contact with each other. A cytoplasm connection is established and plasmids are replicated, then the copy is transferred to the recipient. It is not correct to describe this as 'bacterial sex', nor is it simply the transfer of plasmids, so that one gains and one loses

How does human behaviour speed up antibiotic resistance?

Several examples of ill-advised behaviour in humans helps antibiotic resistance develop faster than it otherwise would:

- We are prescribed and we take antibiotics when we don't need them. Perhaps for a trivial infection that our immune system would clear up anyway, or for an infection that is viral, which cannot be helped by any antibiotic. Either way, the end result is that more bacteria are exposed to antibiotics, creating a selection pressure for individuals that possess resistance alleles. Even in the UK, doctors still over-prescribe and wrongly prescribe antibiotics, but in many parts of the world they are available over the counter, leading to a situation that is almost out of control.

- Patients are also very bad at using antibiotics correctly. We take antibiotics until we feel better, then stop, without completing the whole course. This kills only the weakest bacteria causing the infection. The strongest ones manage to survive when they may well have been killed had the course been completed. When the antibiotic course is not completed, they are granted a reprieve, and can then breed without competition.

- Even worse, we store the leftover antibiotics for the next time we feel ill, and then take half a course without the doctor's prescription. This has similar effects to above, compounded by the fact that out-of-date antibiotics are probably less effective.

- Most significantly of all, is our practice of using antibiotics prophylactically, in other words, as a preventative measure. This does not happen too much in human medicine but it is common practice in agriculture. Animals kept in crowded, high-density living conditions are more susceptible to disease, so antibiotics are used to keep them healthy. Animals treated with antibiotics also tend to grow faster, because they never have to expend any energy or resources fighting off infections, providing a double incentive to farmers. In the UK there are clear guidelines that vets should only prescribe antibiotic therapeutically, to treat a specific illness, but the worldwide situation is more of a problem.

- There is a clear ethical dilemma with the use of antibiotics in farming. On one hand it reduces suffering and promotes health in the animals which leads to a more profitable operation. On the other hand, it speeds up the development of resistance and in some cases may leave the meat contaminated.

3.2.11 Biodiversity may be measured within a habitat

The term diversity describes the extent to which different species form the community of an ecosystem. An ecosystem with a greater number of different species is more diverse than one that contains only a limited number of species.

Ecosystems can show a great range in diversity. Environments such as a coral reef or a rainforest show a high species diversity because conditions are generally favourable and stable. In these situations biotic factors – those due to other organisms – dominate organisms' lives. In contrast, in harsh environments such as the arctic or desert regions, there is low species diversity and abiotic factors dominate, usually temperature and water availability.

Human activity can have an adverse effect on diversity. The following agricultural practices have all been shown to reduce diversity:

- Concentrating on a small number of crops and growing these as large areas of **monoculture**

- Removing hedgerows and field boundaries to make maximum use of land area

- Draining marshy areas and removing unprofitable pockets of woodland

- Using large quantities of chemical fertilisers to obtain maximum yield

- Using pesticides to deal with the increased damage from insects, plant diseases and weeds that are the result of growing large areas of the same crop on the same land for many successive years.

Index of diversity

An **index of diversity** puts a numerical value on the number of species present in an ecosystem. It takes into account the number of individuals in each species in the community, something often called species richness. However, diversity depends not only on richness, but also on evenness. Evenness compares the similarity of the population size of each of the species present.

For the AS/A2 specification, you need to know how to use an index of diversity known as the Simpson's Reciprocal Index. There are many different diversity indices, including other types of the Simpson's index (see below).

Using Simpson's Reciprocal Index

Calculation of Simpson's Reciprocal Index of diversity (d) is possible using the formula:

$$d = \frac{N(N-1)}{\Sigma n(n-1)}$$

where N = total number of organisms of all species
and n = total number of organisms of each species
Σ = sum of all

The value we get represents the probability that, if we randomly choose two individuals, they will belong to distinct species. Thus the minimum value possible, 1, represents no diversity, increasing values represent increasing diversity, with maximum diversity getting 5.

As an example, Table 5 shows the number of different birds in a particular habitat.

Species	Number (n)	(n–1)	n(n–1)
Chaffinch	2	1	2
Great tit	6	5	30
Sparrow	12	11	132
Blue tit	4	3	12
Total	24	20	176

Substituting the data into the above formula

$$d = \frac{24\,(23)}{176} = 3.136$$

So, the diversity of this habitat is sort of medium – it's not high but it's not particularly low either.

Examiners' Notes

You may read about the Simpson's diversity indicies but it will always be Simpson's Reciprocal Index that you are asked about in AS/A2 exams.

How Science Works

In science, we make advances by a combination of two processes:

1 **Observation** We look at the world and say 'Could it possibly be...?' and then come up with testable ideas. We call these **hypotheses**.

2 **Experimentation** We gather evidence and analyse the data to draw reliable conclusions. Sometimes we gather support for our hypothesis, and sometimes we disprove it. Importantly, we never, ever, prove anything. So don't write this in your conclusions.

From your practical investigations in biology you will already be familiar with many of the basic principles used by scientists in their research. The following rules should be applied to any scientific investigation.

Testing a hypothesis

Fig H1 summarises the stages in scientific research.

Progress in science is made when a hypothesis is tested by an experiment. Contrary to popular belief, scientists do not just do experiments to see what

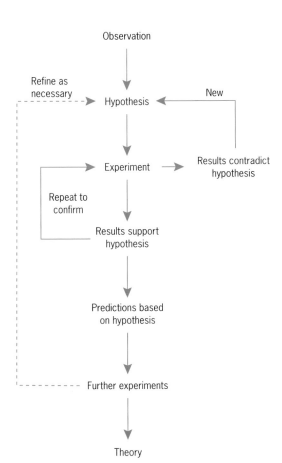

Fig H1
The stages of scientific research

happens. Fun though it might be, they don't just mix chemicals together and watch the results.

An experiment must be designed to test one possible explanation of an observation. The definition of a good hypothesis is that an experiment can either support or disprove it. Strictly, experiments can never prove that a hypothesis is absolutely, definitely correct. There is always the possibility that another explanation, one that no one has thought of, could fit the evidence equally well. However, an experiment can prove that a hypothesis is definitely wrong.

Unfortunately, people are often tempted to bypass the testing stage and go straight to an explanation without obtaining any experimental evidence. Some people seem to be uncomfortable when they are unable to find an explanation for a phenomenon. Even scientists have a tendency to be biased towards finding evidence to support their hypothesis.

As a student, you may well have done an investigation during which you were disappointed to get results that disproved your hypothesis. Or maybe your results were not what you expected. When this happens students often suggest that their experiment has 'gone wrong', but, in scientific research, negative results are just as important as positive ones.

When does a hypothesis become an accepted theory?

A hypothesis only becomes accepted theory when it has been thoroughly tested. The hypothesis may suggest predictions that, in turn, can be tested by further experiments and observations. Other scientists try to think of alternative interpretations of the results. It is normal practice for one scientist to be critical of another's published results. To ensure that published work is of sufficiently high quality, journals practise **peer review** – a submitted paper is reviewed by two or three other experts in the field to make sure the experiments have been carried out well, and that the way the results have been interpreted is reasonable.

Essential Notes

The term 'expert in the field' is used to describe a scientist with experience and a great deal of knowledge in a particular area of science. In peer review, the scientists reviewing their colleagues' (peers') research, need to work in the same area of science, to be able to give a reliable and useful opinion of its quality.

It should also be possible to repeat an experiment and get the same results. Only after many confirmatory experiments is it likely that a new idea will be accepted. For example, for many years it was thought that cell membranes had a structure rather like a sandwich with protein 'bread' and phospholipid 'filling'. After many experiments this hypothesis was shown to be false and it has been replaced by the fluid-mosaic explanation described in this unit. This idea is now so well supported that it is described as the theory of plasma membrane structure.

Once a hypothesis is supported in this way, by many experimental results and observations, it may be accepted as the best explanation of an observation.

A theory is, therefore, a well-established hypothesis that is supported by a substantial body of evidence. The Theory of Natural Selection, for example, is based on huge numbers of observations, predictions and experiments that support the underlying hypothesis.

Designing an investigation

Suppose you are asked to design an experiment to investigate the effect of temperature on the rate of reaction of an enzyme such as catalase.

Your hypothesis could be

Temperature has an effect on the rate of enzyme controlled reactions.

Variables and controls

Catalase breaks down hydrogen peroxide to water and oxygen. To investigate the effect of temperature on the reaction, you could set up water baths at a range of temperatures, mix the catalase and hydrogen peroxide and measure the amount of oxygen released at each temperature.

There are, of course, practical difficulties to be overcome, such as collecting the oxygen without letting any escape, but in principle the experiment is quite simple. The key to this and all similar experiments is that you do three things:

- Select and set up a range of different values for the factor whose effect you are testing, in this case temperature. This factor is the **independent variable**.

- Measure the change in the factor that you are testing, in this case the rate of oxygen production. This is the **dependent variable**.

- Keep all other factors, such as enzyme and hydrogen peroxide concentrations, the same. These are the **controlled variables**.

Including a control experiment

One other precaution is to carry out a **control** experiment. This is not the same as keeping other variables constant. Its purpose is to ensure that changes made to the independent variable have not in themselves changed any other factor, and that the results really are due to the factor being tested.

For example, in the enzyme investigation featured above, how do we know that it is the enzyme that is breaking down the substrate and not simply the effect of temperature, or some other chemical in the enzyme solution? To answer that question, we must do a control experiment in which the enzyme is first boiled (to denature it), or left out altogether. If no oxygen is produced, we have shown that it really was the enzyme that was catalysing the reaction, not another factor.

Another example of a control can be taken from the common practical to test how effectively different antiseptics kill bacteria. Paper discs soaked in the antiseptic might be placed on a bacterial lawn in a Petri dish as shown in Fig H2.

In this experiment four of the discs were soaked in different antiseptics. The fifth disc was the control. The control disc should not be just a plain paper disc, but a disc that has also been soaked in sterile water, or whatever solvent was used in the antiseptics. This would show that the results obtained were really

Examiners' Notes
- The independent variable is the one the experimenter changes. The dependent variable is the one the experimenter measures.
- All other possible variables are kept constant.

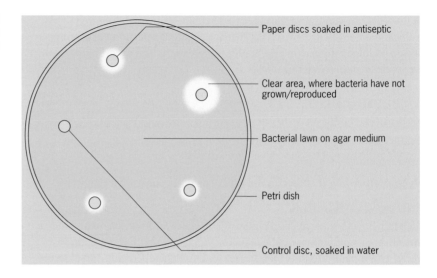

Fig H2
The effect of antiseptic discs on bacteria growth

Paper discs soaked in antiseptic

Clear area, where bacteria have not grown/reproduced

Bacterial lawn on agar medium

Petri dish

Control disc, soaked in water

due to the antiseptics and not, perhaps, to something that could dissolve from the paper disc.

What happens if it is not possible to control all the variables?

Sometimes it is not easy to ensure that all the major factors have been controlled. In an experiment on enzyme activity, controlling all the variables, apart from the independent variable you want to test, is quite straightforward. However, when experimenting with living organisms, investigations are rarely so simple because living things, themselves, are so variable.

If you are measuring the response of an animal to a stimulus, such as a woodlouse to light, you can never be sure that every single woodlouse will respond in the same way. Although most woodlice will move away from light, some might not. Even the simplest of organisms respond to many stimuli. A living thing may behave untypically according to how well fed it is, its age, the time of day, its sexual maturity, or just because it is genetically different from most.

The only way to deal with this uncontrollable variability is to *repeat* an experiment several times and to use a large number of different organisms. Even in an experiment like the one using catalase it would be necessary to repeat the procedure several times for each value of the independent variable. For example, you would make several measurements of rate of oxygen production at 35 °C, several at 40 °C. Each repeat is called a **replicate**. Repetition increases the **reliability** of the results, and this increases the likelihood of being able to draw **valid** conclusions.

For students, there is nearly always a limit to the number of times an experiment can be repeated. Even researchers have time and resource constraints, and it is necessary to use judgement about the likely reliability of a set of data. If the results from replicates are all very similar, it is more likely that the results are reliable.

Accuracy and limitations

There is a limit to the accuracy of any measurement made in the course of an experiment. One limiting factor is the accuracy of the measuring instrument. A second is the care with which the instrument is used. But in biological experiments there is often a practical limit to the accuracy that it is worth trying to achieve. Although instruments exist which can measure length to a fraction of a micrometre, there would be no point in such accuracy when measuring tail length in mice in an investigation of variation. In fact, with a wriggling mouse, it might be difficult to measure even to the nearest millimetre. This difficulty would be compounded by having to decide exactly where the base of the tail actually starts. It is important, therefore, to consider the accuracy that might reasonably be expected from a set of data.

Accuracy is often confused with reliability. Consider the data in Table H1.

Leaf	Loss in mass over 24 hours/g	
	Plant A	Plant B
1	1.03	0.28
2	0.96	0.72
3	0.89	0.74
4	1.05	0.69
5	0.94	0.64
Mean	0.968	0.64

Table H1
Comparing loss in mass of leaves from two different types of plant

Taking measurements from several specimens increases the reliability of the results, but it does not make them more accurate. For plant A, all the results are reasonably similar, which suggests that the value for the mean is probably quite reliable. However, if another five leaves were measured, it is highly unlikely that exactly the same mean would be obtained.

The mean is given to 3 significant figures, but the results only to 2 significant figures. It is clearly absurd to give a value for the mean that is more precise than the accuracy of the measurements. Calculators give answers to many places of decimals, but judgement has to be used about the number of significant figures that can sensibly be given in data for means, or other calculations that are derived by manipulating raw data.

The mean for plant B looks unreliable, to say the least. The result for Leaf 1 is very different from all of the others, so the mean comes well below all the other results. It may be that this result was a mistaken reading of the balance. On the other hand the anomaly may have been because the leaf was atypical: it may have been much smaller, with fewer stomata than normal, or half-dead, for example. Without information about the original masses from which the losses were calculated it is impossible to guess. Expressing the results as percentage loss rather than as total loss would make comparison more reasonable.

Associations and correlations: What affects what?

Many biological investigations depend on a combination of observation and data analysis rather than on actual experiments. This is because it is often not practical to carry out proper controlled experiments with living organisms in the field. There are two reasons for this:

- Logistical reasons. The complexity of interrelationships between organisms and the environment makes it virtually impossible.

- Ethical reasons. It is, for example, not ethical to remove the whole population of one species in an ecosystem in order to find the effect on the food web. Similarly you can't experiment on the effects of smoking by taking two groups of people and making one group smoke and the other group not, while keeping all other factors the same.

Investigators, therefore, have to look for associations that occur in the normal course of events. However, care needs to be taken when drawing conclusions. The number of fish in a lake affected by acid rain or some other pollutant may decline, but this does not necessarily mean that the pollution has caused the decline, or even that the two are connected. Further investigations could look for data on natural populations of particular fish species in water of different acidity. It would also be possible to carry out laboratory experiments to determine fish survival rates in water of different acidity. Results might well show that the lower the pH the lower the survival rate. In this case there would be a correlation between pH and fish survival. This would still not prove that the decline in fish numbers in the lake was actually caused by the acidity.

If you counted, say, the number of nightclubs and pubs and the number of churches in several towns and cities and then plotted a graph of one against the other you would almost certainly find a correlation. But this would obviously not prove that churches cause nightclubs and pubs to be built, or the other way round. The correlation is likely to be the result of a completely separate factor, probably the size of the town or city.

Similarly the decline in fish numbers might be due to some other factor, which might or might not be due to acidity. There could be an indirect association, caused by the effect of acidity on the food supply or the acid-related release of toxic mineral ions. A laboratory experiment would be unable to mimic the complex interaction of abiotic and biotic factors in the real situation of the lake.

Nevertheless, it is only by searching for correlations and investigating them further that biologists can increase their understanding of ecology.

In the next chapter we consider in more detail how correlations in data can be analysed.

Essential Notes

A correlation may be either positive or negative. When one factor increases as another increases it is a positive correlation; when one increases while another decreases it is a negative correlation.

Experiments on humans

This phrase may bring to mind a Frankenstein-like image but, in fact, very many experiments are done with human subjects in biology, to investigate the causes of particular diseases, and to test out potential drugs and treatments.

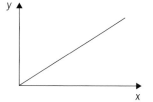

(a) Positive correlation: as x increases, y increases

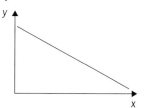

(b) Negative correlation: as x increases, y decreases

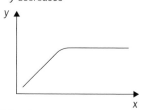

(c) As x increases, y increases up to a point, after which increasing x has no effect

Fig H3
A line graph is a simple way of showing a correlation between two variables. You should be able to look at a graph and describe it in one or two sentences.

Studying human epidemiology

It is just as hard, if not harder, to use experiments to establish links between human diseases and factors such as environmental pollutants, diet, smoking and other aspects of lifestyle as it is to test a woodlouse's response to light for example.

Most associations have been established by studying the incidence of disease or disorders in large groups of people. Looking for patterns in the occurrence of disease in human populations is called **epidemiology**. Many of the suggested links have been controversial and some have caused considerable confusion in the minds of the public. There are still some people who refuse to accept the association between smoking and lung cancer, despite the overwhelming statistical evidence. The stages in establishing the cause of a non-infectious disease are:

- Look for a correlation between a disease and a specific factor.

- Develop hypotheses that could explain how the factor might have its effect.

- Test these hypotheses to find out whether the factor can cause the disease.

Establishing a correlation involves collecting data from very large numbers of people. Because people and their lifestyles are hugely variable, it is important to make comparisons between matched groups as far as possible. For example, suppose you were looking for a correlation between beer drinking and heart disease. It would not be enough just to compare the rates of heart disease between 1000 beer drinkers and 1000 non-drinkers. The ideal comparison would be between groups of people where the only difference in lifestyle was whether or not they drank beer.

In practice this would be virtually impossible to achieve. But, if groups were matched for age, sex, amount of exercise taken and major features of diet, the comparison would be much more valid.

It is very difficult to eliminate the possibility that any correlation is not due to some other linked factor. It may be, for example, that people who like drinking beer also like eating fish and chips, and eat them often. Or, they might have a genetic predisposition to heart disease. The latter is particularly difficult to argue against: those that challenge the evidence linking smoking to lung cancer often use it to put doubt in people's minds.

Once a correlation has been found, the next stage is try to determine how the factor actually causes its effect. This is often much more difficult. Many diseases, such as heart disease and cancers develop as a result of several factors that all interact. The correlation between smoking and incidence of lung cancer has been established for many years but no single specific carcinogen in cigarette smoke has yet been identified. The tar inhaled in cigarette smoke contains a massive cocktail of hundreds of organic compounds. Many of these may have carcinogenic properties, and may affect different people in different ways. Individuals differ in their susceptibility, probably due to genetic factors.

Research on the chemicals in tar, experiments on animals and with tissue cultures, and comparisons between many genetically distinct groupings of people have been done, but the only way to avoid the carcinogenic effects of smoking is never to smoke. One day, if a precise mechanism is discovered, it may be possible to produce non-harmful cigarettes, but this seems remote.

Human clinical trials to test new drugs

Drug testing is an area where good scientific practice is vital. When testing new drugs on human patients, it is not good enough to give some patients the new drug and give nothing to the control group. The patients in the control group should get a pill that is exactly the same as the one with the new drug except for the absence of the active ingredient. A pill without any active ingredient is called a **placebo**.

Clinical trials usually involve **double-blind** investigations. The aim of these is to eliminate subjective bias on the part of both experimental subjects and the experimenters. In a double-blind experiment, neither the individuals nor the researchers know who belongs to the control group and the experimental group. Only after all the data has been obtained do the researchers learn which individuals are which. Performing an investigation in this way lessens the influence of psychological effects, such as prejudices and unintentional physical cues, on the results. Assignment of the subject to the experimental or control group must be done in a random way. The information that identifies the subjects and which group they belonged to is kept by a third party and not given to the researchers until the study is over. Double-blind methods should be applied to any trial where there is the possibility that the results will be affected by conscious or unconscious bias on the part of the experimenter.

Normally, drug trials take place in three phases:

- **A Phase I trial** is an early stage clinical trial in which an experimental drug is tested in a small number of healthy human volunteers to check if it is safe, i.e. there are no side-effects. This type of trial does not test whether a drug works against a particular disease.

- **A Phase II trial** is the next stage clinical trial in which an experimental drug that has successfully passed through a Phase I trial is tested to see if it can treat a specific disease or condition. Human volunteers with the disease or condition are given either the experimental drug or a standard drug, as a control. The groups are then compared to see which drug is the most beneficial.

- **A Phase III trial** has a similar format to a Phase II trial but involves a larger number of human patients – usually hundreds or thousands. A drug must pass successfully through Phase III trials before it can be approved for general use.

Practice exam-style questions

1 The complete life of a cell, the time between one cell division and the next, is known as the cell cycle.

   (a) In what phase of the cell cycle does DNA replication occur?

_____ 1 mark

   (b) Explain why it is essential that DNA replication occurs before mitosis.

_____

_____ 2 marks

In a famous series of experiments in the 1950s, Meselsohn and Stahl showed that DNA replication was semi-conservative. Their basic experiment is outlined below:

Fig E1

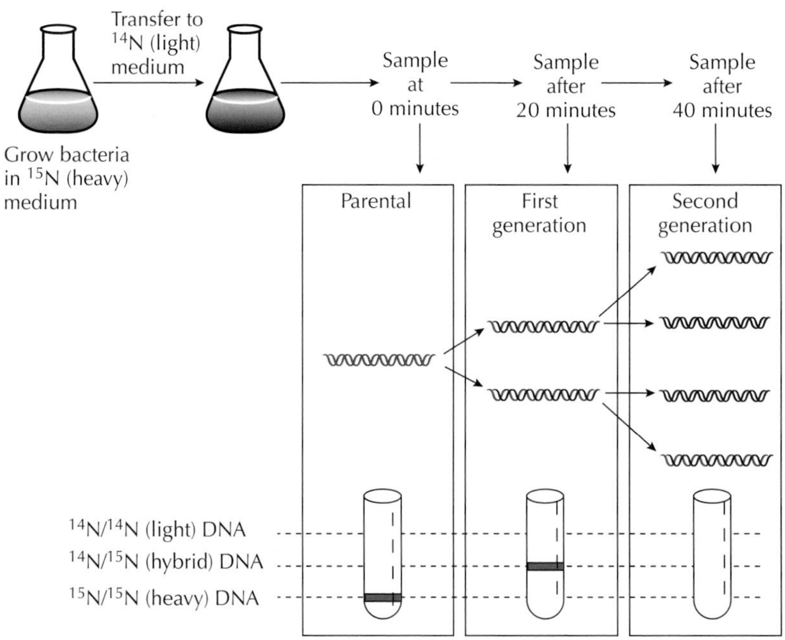

   (c) Explain what is meant by semi-conservative replication.

_____ 1 mark

   (d) Outline the principles behind centrifugation.

_____

_____ 2 marks

   (e) Explain why DNA containing hybrid $^{15}N/^{14}N$ formed a band above that of $^{15}N/^{15}N$.

_____ 1 mark

(f) Complete the diagrams to show the positions of the bands in the second generation. Explain your answer.

_____

_____

_____ 2 marks

Total marks: 9

2 The diagram shows some of the changes as blood flows through different blood vessels.

Fig E2

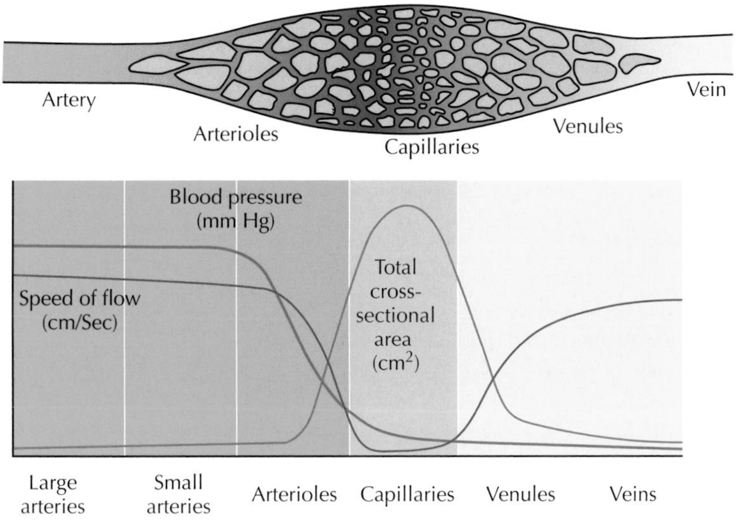

(a) Why are arteries and veins classed as organs but capillaries are not?

_____

_____

_____ 2 marks

(b) (i) Explain why blood pressure is high in the arteries.

_____ 1 mark

(ii) Explain why blood pressure drops as blood flows from the large arteries through the capillaries.

_____

_____ 2 marks

(c) Describe and explain the relationship between total cross-sectional area and speed of flow.

_____

_____

_____ 2 marks

(d) Explain how each of the following contributes to the efficient exchange of substances between blood and tissues:

  (i) The speed of flow.

  (ii) The structure of capillaries.

_____

_____ 2 marks

(e) Give two ways in which the flow of blood through the veins is maintained.

_____

_____ 2 marks

Total marks: 11

3 An Australian study of 14 000 sets of twins was carried out to see if there was any evidence for a genetic basis for homosexuality. They focused on male, identical twins. Of the study subjects that were homosexual, 38% had a twin that was also homosexual.

(a) Explain how identical twins can arise.

_____ 2 marks

(b) Explain why the researchers were interested in identical twins.

_____

_____ 2 marks

(c) Suggest a hypothesis for this investigation.

_____ 1 mark

(d) Suggest a conclusion for this investigation.

_____ 1 mark

(e) Suggest why such as conclusion might not be seen as valid.

_____ 1 mark

Total marks: 7

4 The diagram shows the changes in the DNA content of a cell during cell division.

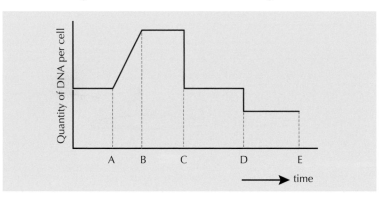

Fig E3

(a) Identify the type of cell division shown in the diagram. Give a reason for your answer.

_____

_____ 2 marks

(b) What is happening in the nucleus between A and B.

_____ 1 mark

(c) What is happening to the cell at point C?

_____ 1 mark

(d) Describe the appearance of the chromosomes between points C and D.

_____

_____

_____ 2 marks

Total marks: 6

5 A student looked at a root tip preparation through a light microscope, and counted the number of cells in each phase of mitosis. The results are shown in the table.

Phase	Number of cells
Interphase	18
Prophase	20
Metaphase	14
Anaphase	4
Telophase	9

(a) How can you tell that this is a rapidly dividing tissue?

_____ 1 mark

(b) Describe what happens to the chromosomes in anaphase.

_____

_____ 2 marks

(c) Suggest why there are so few cells in anaphase.

_____ 1 mark

In a healthy individual, cell division is carefully controlled and cells only divide when they should. At any one time, the vast majority of somatic (body) cells are in interphase.

(d) Describe the appearance of the nucleus of a cell in interphase.

_____ 2 marks

(e) How many chromosomes are present in a human somatic cell?

_____ 1 mark

(f) Explain how mutations in a somatic cell can lead to the development of a tumour.

_____

_____ 3 marks

Total marks:10

6 The table shows the results of a survey into the number of different small mammal species found in two different woodlands.

Species	Number of individuals	
	Woodland A	Woodland B
Woodmouse	15	14
Common shrew	3	8
Bank vole	17	9
Grey squirrel	9	12
Field vole	0	6
Common dormouse	0	2

The formula for diversity (d) is:

$$d = \frac{N\,(N-1)}{\Sigma n\,(n-1)}$$

where N = total number of organisms of all species

and n = total number of organisms of each species

Σ = sum of all

Use this formula to answer the questions.

(a) Explain what is meant by _diversity_ in an ecosystem.

_____

_____ 2 marks

(b) Calculate a diversity index for Woodland A.

_____ 2 marks

(c) Suggest two human activities that could reduce the species diversity in woodland A.

_____

_____ 2 marks

Total marks: 6

7 In an investigation into the properties of haemoglobin, researchers studied two species of Indian geese. The greylag goose lives at sea level all the year round, while the barheaded goose migrates up to Tibet, crossing the Himalayas at heights of up to 9000 metres. At that altitude, the partial pressure of oxygen is much lower than it is at sea level.

The graph shows the oxygen dissociation curve for the barheaded and greylag goose.

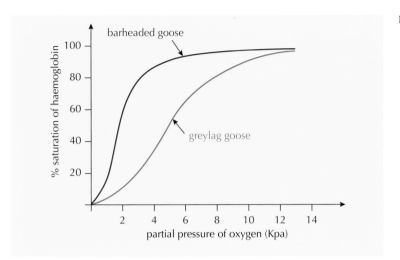

Fig E4

(a) State and explain the differences between the oxygen dissociation curves for the barheaded goose and the greylag goose.

_____

_____ 2 marks

(b) Explain what is meant by the Bohr effect.

_____

_____ 2 marks

(c) Explain the importance of the Bohr effect on the delivery of oxygen to the tissues.

_____

_____ 2 marks

Tubifex, or sludge worms, contain haemoglobin. They live in poorly oxygenated water where they burrow into the mud, head first.

(d) Explain why organisms like tubifex have haemoglobin.

_____ 1 mark

(e) When oxygen concentrations are low, tubifex move out of their tubes and expose more of their bodies to the water. Explain how this helps them to gain oxygen.

_____ 2 marks

_____
Total marks: 9

8 The pig is a fast-growing animal with the potential to achieve more than a hundredfold increase in body weight before the age of 12 months. A piglet weighing 1.5 kg at birth can attain a weight of over 150 kg before its first birthday. The graph shows the growth rate of different body tissues during the pig's first year of life.

Fig E5

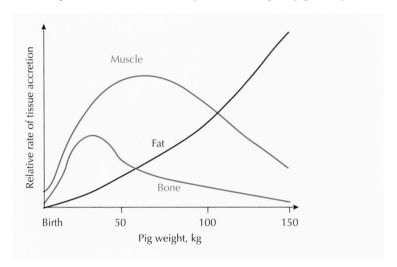

(a) Suggest how breeders could have obtained such fast-growing pigs without the use of artificial growth stimulants.

_____

_____ 2 marks

(b) Use the graph to suggest and explain one problem caused by this rapid growth rate.

_____

_____ 2 marks

Endangered species, such as the giant panda, snow leopard and white rhino have stud books, in which a detailed record is kept on the origin and reproductive history of each captive individual.

(c) Explain what conservationists are trying to achieve by keeping a stud book.

_____

_____

_____

_____ 3 marks

Total marks: 7

9 The use of animals for experimentation has been a controversial topic for many years. Rats are particularly suitable animals. Laboratory rats have been selectively inbred for years in order to produce pure strains, as genetically similar as possible.

(a) Suggest why scientists want to study rats that are genetically similar.

_____

_____ 2 marks

(b) Suggest one problem with inbreeding.

_____ 1 mark

(c) Outline **one** argument for and **one** argument against using animals for experimentation.

_____

_____

_____

_____ 2 marks

Total marks: 5

Answers, explanations, hints and tips

Question	Answer	Marks
1 (a)	Interphase. (S phase is an even more accurate answer.)	1
1 (b)	DNA must double so that each daughter cell gets an equal amount after cell division.	2
1 (c)	In each new DNA molecule, one strand is original and one is new.	1
1 (d)	Mixture is spun in a super gravitational field so that the components separate out according to their density.	2
1 (e)	$^{14}N/^{15}N$ DNA is less dense than $^{15}N/^{15}N$.	1
1 (f)	One band at mid level and one higher up on the N^{14}/N^{14} line. Reason: two of the new strands will be all new/all N^{14}/N^{14} and 2 will be N^{14}/N^{15}	2, 1 for answer, 1 for reason
		Total 9
2 (a)	Capillaries are made from one type of specialised cell and are therefore classed as tissues. Arteries and veins are made from more than one type of specialised cell/tissue and are therefore classed as organs.	2, 1 for each point
2 (b) (i)	They have just received blood from the left ventricles of the heart.	1
2 (b) (ii)	The elastic recoil (or elastic fibres) of the artery and arteriole walls absorbs the pressure/pulse wave.	2
2 (c)	Relationship: the greater the total cross-sectional area, the slower speed of flow. Explanation: there is more resistance to flow through capillaries/more friction between capillary wall and blood.	2, 1 for each point
2 (d) (i)	The slower flow gives more time for exchange/diffusion.	1
2 (d) (ii)	The permeable walls allow efficient exchange. OR Thin walls allow rapid diffusion.	1
2 (e)	Valves prevent backflow. Large lumen minimises friction between blood and vessel wall.	2
		Total 11
3 (a)	One zygote splits (1) develops into two genetically identical embryos (1)	2
3 (b)	Identical twins have the same genes (1) so any differences are likely to be due to environment (1)	2
3 (c)	Hypothesis: Homosexuality is genetically determined.	1
3 (d)	Conclusion: There is no genetic basis to homosexuality.	1
3 (e)	Invalid because the sample was too small.	1
		Total 7
4 (a)	Meiosis: Either: there are two cell divisions, or, the DNA content of the cell is halved.	2
4 (b)	The DNA has replicated/copied itself.	1

Question	Answer	Marks
4 (c)	Cytokinesis/cytoplasmic division.	1
4 (d)	They will be double chromosomes (which means each chromosome consists of 2 chromatids), one from each homologous pair/a single set. (NB they will not be single chromosomes – that doesn't happen until the second meiotic division.)	2
		Total 6
5 (a)	Short interphase, or, interphase only as long as prophase.	1
5 (b)	Any two from: Chromatids are pulled apart; By the spindle fibres; One set of chromatids moves to each pole.	2, 1 for each point
5 (c)	It is quick/the shortest phase.	1
5 (d)	Any 2 from: No visible chromosomes; No spindle; DNA exists as chromatin; Nuclear membrane present.	2
5 (e)	46 (or 23 pairs)	1
5 (f)	Any three from: Genes that control cell division/oncogenes mutate; Tumour supressor genes mutate; Cell loses control of cell division; Mitosis out of control; Mass of cells/tissue develops.	3, 1 for each point
		Total 10
6 (a)	A measure of the number of different species (1) in relation to the number of individuals (1).	2
6 (b)	3.38	2
6 (c)	Any two from: Removal of hedgerows; Monoculture; Pesticide spraying; Human activity/trampling; Deforestation	2, 1 for each point
		Total 6
7 (a)	Barheaded goose haemoglobin has a *higher affinity* for oxygen. It can, therefore, bind to O_2 even at low partial pressures.	2
7 (b)	Any two from: Carbon dioxide reduces the affinity of haemoglobin for oxygen; Carbon dioxide makes haemoglobin give up its oxygen; Carbon dioxide is acidic/acid de-stabilises Hb; Curve moves to the right.	2, 1 for each point

Question	Answer		Marks
7 (c)	Oxygen will be released into the respiring tissue that needs it most.		2
7 (d)	To store oxygen in conditions of low oxygen tension.		1
7 (e)	Greater surface area (1) for absorption of oxygen (1).		2
			Total 9
8 (a)	Any two from:		
	By selective breeding; Breed together the fastest growing individuals/ those with genes for rapid growth; For several/many generations.		2, 1 for each point
8 (b)	Any two from: Muscle and fat grows faster than bone; Bones/joints can't support weight of animal; Animals suffer/are lame/grow in a deformed way.		2, 1 for each point
8 (c)	Any three from: Stud books try to avoid/minimise inbreeding; Fewer individuals with genetic defects; Promote heterozygosity; Maintain healthy gene pool.		3, 1 for each point
			Total 7
9 (a)	It controls an important variable	(1)	2, 1 for each point
	and it allows us to draw valid conclusions	(1).	
9 (b)	High proportion of genetic abnormalities.		1
9 (c)	For Allows us to develop medicines that are safe for humans and for other animals; Alleviates suffering; Reduces need for tests on humans. Against: Waste of life; Unnecessary suffering; Assumes that the needs of humans are more important than those of another species.		2, 1 for a 'for' point and 1 for an 'against' point
			Total 5

Glossary

Accuracy	**HSW** A measure of how close the data is to the actual true value. Note the difference between accuracy and precision. If a man is 1.81 m tall, a measurement of 1.743 m is precise but not accurate. The difference between accurate and precise is illustrated below:

Precise-Accurate

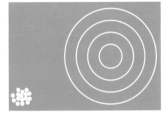

Precise-Inaccurate

Imprecise-Accurate

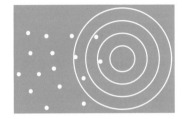

Imprecise-Inaccurate

Affinity	Degree of attraction. For example, haemoglobin has a high affinity for oxygen.
Allele	An alternative form of a gene. For example, a flower colour gene could have an allele for red flowers and one for white flowers.
Amylopectin	One of the two polysaccharides that makes up starch. A branched polymer of glucose.
Amylose	One of the two polysaccharides that makes up starch. An unbranched polymer of glucose.
Anaphase	Phase of mitosis in which the chromatids split (at the centromere) and are pulled to opposite poles by the spindle fibres.
Anomalous result	Measurement that falls outside the normal range of values. When many repeats are made, anomalous data can be identified more easily.
Antibiotic	An anti-bacterial drug such as penicillin, tetracycline.
Apoplast pathway	Pathway taken by water travelling through the outer surface of the root to the xylem in the centre of the root. Water moves through the gaps *between* cells, as opposed to the **symplast pathway**.
Archaea	In classification, one of the three domains, along with Bacteria and Eukarya. Once thought to be bacteria, Archaea are single-celled organisms without nuclei and with membranes that are different from all other organisms. They have a unique tough outer cell wall and protective enzymes that allow them to thrive in extreme conditions such as the hot/acidic waters.
Artificial selection	Selective breeding, where human activity directs natural selection. Seen in many domestic species such as dogs, cows, wheat.
Bacteria	Simple, single-celled prokaryotic organism. Bacteria can be classed as one of the three domains. See also **Archaea** and **Eukarya**.
Bactericidal	Substance/agent that kills bacteria.
Bacteriostatic	Substance/agent that prevents bacteria from reproducing rather than killing them.
Basal metabolic rate	The rate of respiration at rest, when the body is 'ticking over'. Measured in oxygen consumption or heat production.

Base	In nucleic acids (DNA and RNA), one of four nitrogen-containing compounds, that fit together like jigsaw pieces. In DNA there are Adenine, Thymine, Guanine and Cytosine (C bonds to G, A to T). RNA has Uracil (U) instead of Thymine.
Benign	A non-cancerous tumour.
Binomial	Having two names: the current classification system of species is binomial, for example, *Homo sapiens*.
Biodiversity	In conservation, a measure of the number of different species in a particular ecosystem. The influence of humans often reduces biodiversity.
Blind trial	**HSW** A trial in which the patient does not know whether they have been given the active drug or the inactive control (placebo). See also **double-blind trial**.
Bohr effect	Name given to the fact that in the presence of carbon dioxide, the affinity of haemoglobin for oxygen is lower.
Bottleneck	See **genetic bottleneck**.
Carbonic anhydrase	Enzyme that speeds up the reaction between carbon dioxide and water, forming carbonic acid, which then dissociates into H^+ and HCO_3^- ions. Particularly important in red blood cells, where the H^+ ions cause haemoglobin to release O_2.
Carcinogen	Cancer-causing agent.
Casparian strip	Layer of waterproof material around the endodermis in a plant root. Its function is to block the apoplast pathway.
Cellulase	Enzyme that breaks down cellulose.
Cellulose	Unbranched polymer of β glucose. Forms long chains that bond to parallel chains via hydrogen bonds, forming fibres of great strength. Found in plant cell walls. Major component of paper, wood and cotton.
Cell wall	Outer protective coat secreted by cells of certain organisms. Plants always have cell walls made of cellulose.
Centromere	The point of attachment of two chromatids on a double chromosome.
Chemotherapy	Using drugs to treat cancer.
Chiasmata	In meiosis, the points of crossover. In other words, sites where chromosomes break and join to others.
Chloroplast	Plant organelle that is the site of photosynthesis. Internal membrane system (grana) provides a large surface area to house chlorophyll.
Chromatid	One half of a double chromosome (present at the start of cell division).
Chromatin	'Spread out' DNA in the nucleus of a non-dividing cell.
Chromosome	Condensed mass of DNA that appears just before cell division. Each chromosome is one super-coiled DNA molecule containing thousands of genes.
Clone	An identical genetic copy. It is possible to clone DNA strands, cells or whole organisms.
Cohesion tension	Mechanism by which water passes up the xylem of a plant, from roots to leaves. The cohesion of water allows continuous columns under great tension.
Conjugation	Mechanism of gene transfer between bacteria in direct contact with each other. Involves copying and transfer of plasmids. For example, genes for antibiotic resistance can be passed from one species to another. An example of horizontal gene transfer.

Constrict	To get smaller, as in vasoconstrict, when an arteriole gets narrower. NB: Only arterioles can do this, not veins, arteries or capillaries.
Continuous variation	Variation that can be any value within a range, for example, height, shoe size. Tends to be controlled by many alleles (polygenic) and environmental factors that combine to give the phenotype.
Control	**HSW** A supplementary experiment performed as a comparison, to control the variables. An important way of validating an experiment.
Controlled variables	**HSW** The variables that are kept constant during an experiment.
Countercurrent system	When fluid flows in parallel tubes in opposite directions. Maximises efficiency of material exchange by maintaining a diffusion gradient along the whole length of the system. Maximises gas exchange in fish gills.
Crossover	In meiosis, the process that swaps blocks of genes between homologous chromosomes. Creates new combinations of alleles, so increasing variation.
Dependent variable	**HSW** The variable that is measured as it changes during an experiment.
Dicotyledons	The largest group of flowering plants. Often shortened to dicot.
Differentiation	When a stem cell becomes specialised, for example, as a nerve, muscle or epithelial cell. Happens by the selective activation of genes.
Diffusion	Molecular mixing, where particles in a gas or liquid move from an area of high concentration to an area of lower concentration until evenly spread.
Dilate	To get larger, as in vasodilate, when an arteriole expands its diameter.
Diploid	A cell/organism which contains two sets of chromosomes. Shown as 2n. For example, in humans, 2n = 46. See also **haploid**.
Discontinuous variation	Variation that falls neatly into categories; one thing or the other, for example, ABO blood groups. Tends to be controlled by single alleles, which are present or not.
Dissociation	Dis-association, in other words, coming apart. For example, when haemoglobin gives up its oxygen, or when an acid gives up an H^+ ion.
Diversity	A measure of the number of different species in a community.
Dizygotic twins	Non-identical, arising from two separate zygotes.
DNA	Deoxyribonucleic acid.
DNA hybridisation	Technique that estimates the evolutionary closeness of different species by comparing the similarity of their DNA sequences.
DNA polymerase	Key enzyme in DNA replication. Catalyses the addition of complementary nucleotides on the exposed strands.
DNA replication	The copying of DNA molecules. The two strands unwind and act as templates for the creation of two identical copies. Tales place in interphase, before cell division.
Domain	Over-arching group in classification, above kingdom. See **Archaea**, **Bacteria** and **Eukarya**.
Dominant	An allele which, if present, is shown in the phenotype.
Double blind trials	**HSW** Trials in which neither the patients nor the researchers know who is getting the active drug and who is getting the control (placebo). Done to eliminate bias, so increasing the validity of the results.

Ectotherm	'Heat from outside', in other words, cold blooded. All animals except mammals and birds are ectotherms.
Endodermis	Means literally 'inner skin'. In plants, a layer of cells around the vascular tissue (xylem and phloem). Endodermal cells in roots are surrounded by the Casparian strip.
Endotherm	'Heat from within', in other words, warm blooded animal. Mammals and birds are endotherms.
Epidermis	Means literally 'outer skin'. A protective layer of cells.
Eukarya	The domain that contains the eukaryotes; animals, plants, fungi and protoctists. See also **Archaea**, **Bacteria**.
Eukaryotic cell	Cells with a true nucleus and DNA organised into chromosomes. Complex cell with organelles such as mitochondria, endoplasmic reticulum, and so on. Animals, plants and fungi are eukaryotic.
Expressed	A gene is expressed when it is active and being used to make a particular protein/polypeptide.
Exons	In a gene, the base sequences that are expressed, so used to make a polypeptide/protein. See also **introns**.
Founder effect	A situation where a population is founded by just a few individuals, who are not representative of the gene pool from which they came.
Gamete	A sex cell: sperm in males, eggs in females.
Gene	A length of DNA that codes for one protein or polypeptide.
Gene transmission	Vertical gene transmission involves passing genes on from one generation to the next, a fundamental part of reproduction. Horizontal gene transmission is where genes are passed from one species to another. Common in bacteria and some plants.
Generic name	Name of the genus; first part of a scientific name. Always has capital: for example, *Homo* in *Homo sapiens*.
Genetic bottleneck	Situation when a population recovers from a small number of individuals. The new population is likely to show low variation since many alleles have been lost from the gene pool.
Genetic code	The base sequence of the DNA molecule. The code is copied onto molecules of mRNA and used as a template to make polypeptides/proteins.
Genome	The entire DNA sequences contained within the genetic material of an organism. The human genome consists of 3 billion base pairs; 30 000 genes on the 23 chromosomes, plus the non-coding DNA between the genes.
Genotype	The alleles that an organism has. Aa or AA, AaBb or Aabb and so on. Compare with **phenotype**.
Genus	Taxonomic grouping, more general than species but more specific than family. First part of the scientific name. For example, Felis is the genus in *Felis cattus* (cat).
Gill filaments	Supporting structures found in gills. In bony fish, four pairs of gill arches support many gill filaments, which in turn support the gill lamellae.
Gill lamellae	Small flat respiratory surfaces on gill filaments, the equivalent of alveoli in lungs.
Glycogen	Main storage carbohydrate in animals. A highly branched polymer of α glucose, similar to amylopectin. Particularly abundant in liver and muscles.

Growth phase	Part of interphase, which is, in turn, part of the cell cycle. In the G1 phase the cell increases in size as it makes new organelles and cytoplasm. If the cell is going to divide there is a second growth phase, G2, in which it makes enzymes and other proteins essential to cell division.
Haemoglobin	Protein found in the red blood cells of vertebrates, and in the body tissues of some invertebrates. Key function; storage and transport of oxygen; it binds to oxygen when abundant, and releases it when levels are low.
Haploid	A cell/organism that has a single set of chromosomes, for example, human eggs and sperm. Shown as n. For example, in human gametes, n = 23.
Helicase	Class of enzyme that unwinds and separates the two strands of DNA prior to replication or transcription.
Hemicellulose	Molecules made from short chains of β glucose. Helps to bind together the large cellulose fibres in the cell wall.
Heterozygous	Possessing two different alleles. Written as Aa or Bb.
Hierarchy	In taxonomy, a layered system of groups within groups, with no overlap.
Histone	Class of protein that organises the DNA in the nucleus. DNA winds round a histone, like cotton round a bobbin.
Homeostasis	The maintenance of more or less stable conditions within the body. For example, temperature, blood glucose, pH, water potential.
Homologous chromosomes	A pair of chromosomes that have the same genes in the same places (loci) although not always the same alleles. Human females have 23 homologous pairs, while males have 22, because the X and Y chromosomes are not homologous.
Homozygous	Possessing two alleles the same, for example, AA or aa. Said to be 'true breeding'.
Horizontal gene transmission	The transfer of genes from one organism to another that is not its offspring. In practice this usually means gene transfer between individuals of different species. This is common in bacteria, and is thought to be responsible for the spread of antibiotic resistance. See also **vertical gene transmission**.
Humidity	The amount of water vapour in the air. The lower the humidity, the greater the water potential gradient between a wet surface and the air, and the faster the rate of evaporation. Important in sweating (animals) and in transpiration (plants).
Hydrostatic pressure	The physical pressure of fluid. Defined in biology as: Force per unit area exerted by a fluid (such as blood) against a vessel wall.
Hypothesis	**HSW** An idea that it is possible to test by experiment.
Inbreeding	The breeding of genetically similar individuals such as brothers and sisters. It promotes homozygosity and increases the chance of genetic disease.
Incomplete dominance	When two alleles are both expressed in the phenotype. For example, when red and white snapdragon plants are bred together, the offspring are pink.
Independent assortment	A key feature of meiosis, which separates the homologous chromosomes so that any one of a pair of alleles can pass into a gamete with one from any other pair.
Independent variable	**HSW** The variable that is tested during an experiment.
Index of Diversity	A numerical value that reflects the number of different **Index of Diversity** species in a community, in relation to the number of individuals. Used to compare the difference in diversity between two communities, or the change in a community over time.

Interphase	Part of the cell cycle – the period between mitotic divisions.
Interspecific	Between different species. Applies to competition and variation.
Intraspecific	Between members of the same species. Applies to competition and variation.
Introns	Non-coding DNA within a gene. Introns must be removed before translation. See also **exons**.
KPCOFGS	The taxonomic hierarchy; kingdom, phylum, class, order, family, genus, species.
Locus	The position of a gene on a chromosome (plural = loci).
Lymph	Fluid that flows in lymph vessels, which form a network called the lymphatic system. Similar to tissue fluid, but with more lipids and large proteins.
Malignant	A cancerous tumour. Tends to grow at the edges and invade surrounding tissue.
Mass flow	The movement of large volumes of fluid within tubes. An efficient transport system for large organisms.
Meiosis	Cell division that shuffles the genes on the chromosomes so that no two gametes are the same. One diploid cell gives rise to *four* haploid cells.
Metabolic rate	The rate of metabolism, which is basically the same as the rate of respiration. Measured in oxygen consumption/heat production, per unit of mass per unit of time.
Metaphase	Phase in mitosis where the chromosomes can be seen in the middle/equator of the spindle. Remember: meta = middle.
Metastasis	Process in which cancerous cells break off from a malignant tumour and set up secondary tumours elsewhere in the body.
Microfibril	Literally, small fibre. Commonly applies to a bundle of cellulose or protein fibres. Examples of protein microfibrils include the tail of sperm, flagella, cilia and spindle fibres.
Microorganism	Any organism too small to see with the naked eye. Applies to bacteria, algae, yeast and various protoctists such as amoeba.
Mitosis	Standard cell division. One diploid cell gives rise to two identical diploid cells.
Molecular phylogeny	Process in which evolutionary relationships are worked out based on similarity in nucleic acids and proteins. The more base/amino acid sequences in common, the closer the relationship.
Monoculture	Agricultural practice of growing just one crop, often in large fields created by removing hedgerows. Makes economic sense but reduces biodiversity.
Monozygotic twins	Identical twins, arising from one zygote that splits.
MRSA	Methicillin resistant *Staphylococcus aureus*, a strain of bacterium that is resistant to the antibiotic methicillin.
Multiple repeats	Repeated sequences of DNA found in non-coding regions of genome, between genes. Forms the basis for genetic profiling.
Mutation	A change in the genetic material of an organism. A gene mutation is a change in the base sequence of a gene, which will probably result in a change in the amino acid sequence. In turn, this may affect the overall shape and, therefore, the functioning of the protein. Mutation is the ultimate source of all variation.

Normal distribution	Pattern of distribution, which shows as a bell-shaped curve on a graph, in which most values fall in the middle, with fewer at the extremes.
Nucleic acid	Class of organic molecules that includes DNA and the various types of RNA. So called because they are weakly acidic and (originally thought to be) found in the nucleus. All contain nucleotides.
Nucleotide	Basic sub unit of a nucleic acid, consisting of a sugar (deoxyribose or ribose), a phosphate and one of four bases.
Oncogene	A gene that causes cancer. Normal, *proto-oncogenes* control cell division. If they mutate, they become oncogenes. See also **tumour suppressor genes**.
Organ	Collection of tissues that work together to achieve a specific physiological function. For example, kidney, heart, leaf, gill.
Outbreeding	The breeding of genetically different individuals. This increases diversity (or heterozygosity) and reduces the incidence of genetic defects as faulty alleles are usually masked by healthy ones.
Oxygen dissociation curve	Graph that shows the properties of haemoglobin. The x-axis shows the oxygen tension (basically; the amount of oxygen available) and the y-axis shows the % saturation of haemoglobin with oxygen. The further to the left the curve is, the greater the affinity of Hb for oxygen.
Pedigree	Of known ancestry (a 'family tree'). Applies to humans as well as animals.
Perrenation	Survival from one year to the next. Daffodil bulbs and potato tubers are organs of perrenation.
Phenotype	The observable features of an organism (genotype + environment = phenotype). Compare with **genotype**.
Phloem	One of two main types of conducting tissue in plants (see **xylem**). Phloem carries the products of photosynthesis from where they are made ('sources', usually leaves or storage organs) to where they are needed ('sinks', such as growing points, flowers, fruits). This process is called translocation.
Phylogenetic	In taxonomy, from origin of phyla: what evolved from what? A phylogenetic tree shows evolutionary history.
Placebo	**HSW** A sham or fake drug given to people in the control group of a clinical trial.
Plasma	The fluid component of blood, not the cells.
Plasmid	Tiny circles of DNA found in the cytoplasm of bacteria. Contain useful rather than essential genes.
Polygenic	Controlled by many alleles (see **continuous variation**). For example, height in humans.
Polymer	Large organic molecule formed by combining many smaller molecules (monomers) in a regular pattern. Polysaccharides, proteins and nucleic acids are all polymers. In biology, polymers are made by condensation reactions and split by hydrolysis.
Polynucleotide	A polymer of nucleotides, for example, DNA and RNA.
Polypeptide	A chain of amino acids that will fold and bend into a particular shape. Proteins are made from one or more polypeptides.

Polyploid	A cell/organism that has many sets of chromosomes. Wheat plants can, for example, have eight sets of chromosomes.
Potometer	A device that measures transpiration (water loss) from a leafy shoot.
Precision	**HSW** The closeness of repeated measurements to one another. Precision involves choosing the right apparatus and using it properly. Precise readings are not necessarily **accurate** (close to the true value). A faulty piece of equipment or incorrectly used apparatus may give very precise readings (all repeated values are close together) but inaccurate (not true) results. For example, in an experiment with a colorimeter, using a dirty or scratched cuvette (sample tube) might give precise readings, but they will be highly inaccurate.
Primers	Short sections of RNA that attach to a gene before transcription or replication. They show polymerase enzymes where to begin reading the DNA template.
Prokaryotic cell	Simple cells with no true nucleus or complex organelles. Bacteria are prokaryotic.
Proofreading enzymes	Enzymes that check for base-pairing mistakes in DNA replication. They move along the new strand after DNA polymerase, removing any incorrect bases. This minimises the chances of mutations.
Prophase	First stage of mitosis, in which chromosomes condense, the spindle develops and the nuclear membrane disappears.
Protein synthesis	Two-stage process. The first phase is transcription: the base sequence on a gene is copied to make a molecule of mRNA. The second phase is translation: the base sequence on the mRNA is used to assemble amino acids in the right order to make a polypeptide/protein.
Protoctist	One of the four eukaryote kingdoms (along with plants, animals and fungi). Contains algae (including seaweeds), sponges and various unicellular organisms such as amoeba and plasmodium (the malaria-causing organism).
Protoplast	A cell that has lost its cell wall, or has had it removed. Usually a plant cell, but can be bacteria or fungi. Usually done deliberately to allow manipulation/transformation in genetic engineering.
Pulmonary circulation	The circulation through the *lungs* and back to the heart. Contrast with the **systemic circulation**, which carries blood around the rest of the body.
Radiotherapy	Treatment of cancer using radiation.
Random errors	**HSW** Inaccurate values lying equally above or below a true value. Can occur for many reasons, including not following a standard procedure, for example, when measuring out volumes; or using a different batch of enzyme or yeast for repeats.
Random fertilisation	The fact that any egg can be fertilised by any sperm. Another important source of variation, along with crossover and independent assortment.
Re-anneal	To re-join. Seen in DNA hybridisation where the strands are heated so they come apart, are mixed with strands from other species and then re-anneal, forming hybrid DNA.
Recessive	An allele that only appears in the phenotype if the dominant allele is absent. For example, *aa*.
Reliable	**HSW** If a measurement or test is reliable, it gives consistent results each time the activity is repeated. When undertaking an investigation a large number of repeats

	should ideally be taken, and any readings that vary considerably from the others (anomalous results) should be repeated.
Replicate	**HSW** A repeat: An experiment that is repeated is a replicate experiment.
Replication	Making a copy. See **DNA replication**.
Respiration	Universal process in which energy is released from organic molecules such as glucose or lipid, and transferred to ATP so that the cell has instant energy.
Ribosome	A small organelle, the site of protein synthesis.
RNA polymerase	Enzyme that catalyses the addition of complementary nucleotides during transcription.
Root hair cells	Specialised epidermal cell in a plant root. Increases the surface area for the absorption of water and mineral ions.
Root pressure	One of the two forces that move water up a plant, the other being cohesion tension. Root pressure is more significant in small plants, but not powerful enough to force water up to the tops of trees.
Synthesis phase (S phase)	In interphase, the time in which the DNA replicates before cell division.
Scientific name	Two-part name, usually from Latin or Greek, given to each species. For example, *Homo sapiens*. Should always be underlined or in italics.
Selective activation	Selection process in which some genes are active while others are inactive. All cells in an organism contain the same genes, so the key to cell specialisation is the selective activation of specific genes. This is a hugely complex process and underlies cell differentiation and development of the embryo.
Semi-conservative	The mechanism of DNA replication. In each new molecule, one strand is original (it has been conserved) and one strand is new. This was shown by Meselsohn and Stahl's experiment.
Sense strand	The side of the DNA molecule (in a gene) that is used as the template for making the RNA which is then used as a template to make a polypeptide or protein.
Somatic cell	Any cell of a plant or animal other than a germ cell (gamete). In animals somatic cells are diploid, germ cells are haploid.
Specific name	Name of the species; second part of Latin name. No capital: *sapiens*
Spiracle	In the gas exchange system of insects, the opening of a trachea, through which oxygen enters the body and carbon dioxide is expelled.
Standard deviation	A measure of the spread of data about the mean.
Starch	Main storage carbohydrate in plants. See **amylose** and **amylopectin**.
Stem cell	Cell with the ability to differentiate into various specialised cells.
Stomata	Pores, mainly found on the underside of a leaf. They allow gas exchange.
Sugar	Simple carbohydrate. Sugars are sweet, soluble white solids. For example, glucose, sucrose, maltose.
Superbug	Media term for bacteria that are resistant to a variety of antibiotics.
Symplast pathway	Pathway taken by water through a plant root from the outside to the xylem in the centre. Water moves through the living cytoplasm within cells, as opposed to the **apoplast pathway**.

System	Group of organs working together. For example, digestive system.
Systematic errors	**HSW** Values that differ from the true value by the same amount. Systematic errors may occur due to incorrectly calibrated equipment or a fault in the experimental procedure used. For example, using a dirty or scratched cuvette (sample tube) in a colorimeter, the error introduced would be the *same*, or *systematic*, throughout the investigation.
Systemic circulation	Circulation of blood around the body and back to the heart. See also **pulmonary circulation**.
Taxonomy	The science of classification.
Telophase	In mitosis, the final stage of nuclear division, before cytokinesis. Cells in telophase have two separate nuclei, because the two sets of chromatids have reached the poles.
Thermo regulation	Temperature control. See **endotherm** and **ectotherm**.
Tissue	A collection of similar specialised cells that work together. Four main tissues types in the human body are muscle, nerve, epithelia and connective tissue.
Tissue fluid	Fluid that surrounds and nourishes living cells. Formed by filtration of the plasma through the permeable capillary wall. Composition similar to plasma but without the larger proteins.
Totipotent	A stem cell that is capable of differentiating into any of the different specialised cell types. Found in the very early embryo.
Trachea	A large, supported tube in the tracheal system of insects. Mammals also have a trachea (windpipe).
Tracheal system	The gas exchange system of an insect. Basically a system of branching tubes that takes air from the outside to individual cells in the insect's body.
Tracheoles	Tiny permeable tubes that allow gas exchange between air and individual cells in an insect's body. See also **spiracles**, **trachea**. Tracheoles are permeable, trachea are not.
Transcription	The copying of a gene. Takes place in nucleus.
Translation	Using the gene copy made during transcription to assemble a protein. Takes place on a ribosome.
Transpiration	The loss of water (by evaporation) from the surface of a leaf. Most water is lost through stomata on the underside surface of leaves.
Transpiration stream	The flow of water and dissolved ions from the soil, through the plant and out into the atmosphere.
Triplet	In DNA, a group of three bases that codes for a particular amino acid. Also called a codon.
True breeding	Homozygous individuals that always produce offspring of the same type.
Tumour	A swelling caused when cells divide out of control. See also **benign** and **malignant**.
Tumour suppressor gene	Gene coding for a protein that prevents tumour formation. Acts as backup if the proto-oncogenes mutate. If the tumour suppressor genes also mutate, a tumour is much more likely to develop.

Turgid	A pressurised plant cell. Most plant cells absorb water until the vacuole swells and pushes out against the cell wall, which resists any further expansion.
Vacuole	Fluid filled organelle in some cells. Particularly important in plant cells where it stores substances and provides turgor. See also **turgid**
Validity	**HSW** The confidence that researchers put in a set of results and the conclusions drawn from those results. Results are valid if they measure what they are supposed to, and if they are *precise, accurate and reliable* (repeatable). Valid results are obtained through precise, repeatable measurements or observations, made with apparatus and experimental procedures that are suitable for the task.
Vascular system	A transport system in which fluid is moved around the organism in a system of tubes. Also called a mass flow system.
Vascular tissue	Tissue that contains tubes. Xylem and phloem in plants. Blood vessels in animals.
Vertical gene transmission	Gene transfer from one generation to the next, as opposed to **horizontal gene transmission**.
Water potential	A measure of the tendency of a cell or solution to gain water by osmosis. Always a negative scale. Pure water has a water potential of zero.
Xylem	Specialised conducting (= vascular) tissue in plants. Consists of dead hollow cells with strong walls made from lignin and cellulose. Function is to transport water and dissolved minerals from roots to leaves – the transpiration stream.
Zygote	A fertilised egg.

Index

Notes

Notes

Notes